THE STAFFORDSH
A HISTORY

THE STAFFORDSHIRE OATCAKE

A HISTORY

PAMELA SAMBROOK

Ode to the Oatcake
Let us pay homage to the Oatcake
Or woodcake as the old men called them
The oatcake is not a cake at all really
Not like the fairy cake or the Eccles cake
Not a cake in that way
More of a Potteries Poppadum
A sort of Tunstall Tortilla
A clay suzette

Arthur Berry

*The first edition of this book was published with the generous sponsorship
of the Trustees of the Jack Leighton Trust*

The Staffordshire Oatcake a history

Copyright © Pamela Sambrook, 2009

First edition, 2009; reprinted 2009

Published by Palatine Books,
an imprint of Carnegie Publishing Ltd
Carnegie House,
Chatsworth Road,
Lancaster, LA1 4SL
www.carnegiepublishing.com

ISBN 978-1-874181-63-7

Designed and typeset by Carnegie Book Production
Printed and bound in the UK in association with Jellyfish Solutions Ltd

ONE

Introduction
A lifelong interest

EATING STAFFORDSHIRE OATCAKES FOR SUNDAY BREAKFAST is one of my earliest memories, from a childhood in Newcastle-under-Lyme and the Potteries. The size of a breakfast plate and soft, our version of the oatcake was warmed in the oven between two plates and rolled up on the side of our cooked breakfast, soaking up the bacon fat, soft in the centre and often a bit crunchy at the rim. The delicious smell can still take me back to Sundays in the 'forties and 'fifties as effectively as those evocative signature tunes of 'Family Favourites' and 'The Billy Cotton Band Show'.

My interest in oatcakes no doubt dates from these early days, but my love of the Pennine moorlands, the original home of oatcakes, developed a few years later when I was about 18. I became interested in geology and I would spend days walking the Staffordshire moorlands to the north of the Potteries, wading up streams to follow the coal measures and bloodying my knees on the unforgiving gritstone edges. Once, frighteningly, I was caught out by a sudden late-spring blizzard at Royal Cottage, to be rescued from driving snow by a man in a very smelly dry-cleaning van. Little did I realise then that the two interests – oatcakes and the moorlands – were closely related. The warmth and comfort of Sunday

Oatcake country – the rural version. The misty outline of Hen Cloud, one of the gritstone outcrops on the moors at the southern edge of the Pennines, the home of oatcakes.
(Potteries Museum. Photograph William Blake)

breakfast seemed a long way from those stony hillsides and meagre soils to the north, and from the rain that came sweeping down the valleys and sliced into your face.

Years later in 1970, when I was learning to be a museum curator, I had to design and research a project on some aspect of ordinary peoples' lives in the past, as part of a training course. I thought, why not try to explore the traditions of the Staffordshire oatcake and how it has changed over time? Inspired by visits to some of the great oral folk-life archives in Wales and Scandinavia, I put an advert in the local newspaper, *The Evening Sentinel*, asking people to contact me with their memories. I had twenty-six replies, some from the Potteries but some also from further north, from the Pennine fringes. Twenty-six was all I needed, because once you are started on such a search you get passed on by word of mouth. So off I set with a great cumbersome tape recorder and an old camera, the latter soon replaced by the companionship of a friend who was a professional photographer, Cliff Guttridge. I was diffident, almost secretive about all this. The practice if not the idea of 'oral history', as it came to be known later, was relatively new in England at that time. 'Real' historians sat in book-lined libraries and looked at you over the tops of their spectacles, not on a sofa asking daft questions and drinking home-made wine which had the thickness and colour of advocaat.

At last, in 1974, I completed an article for the journal *Folk Life* and published a little booklet.[1] Thirty-odd years later, in autumn 2007, I decided to revisit these researches, as I had found new evidence in the intervening years and a number of friends were asking me about a reprint. No sooner had I begun to reorganise this material than a row blew up in *The Sentinel* about the impending destruction of a traditional oatcake-maker's shop in Hanley, due to be demolished as part of the urban renewal scheme for the Potteries. As a result of this public discussion and the good offices of the newspaper I was able to contact a new group of informants and memories, some face-to-face, some through letters and email.

I met many interesting people during these explorations, both in the 1970s and more recently. Thirty years ago I was welcomed into moorland farmhouse kitchens that were so clean you hardly dared breathe in them – where everything that didn't move was either polished or whitewashed. Yet I did at least realise what a tough way of life the moorlands offered. It is bad enough in the modern winter, but imagine the intense isolation of previous generations, with no cars, no telephones, no electricity, no running water and a dry earth closet down the garden. How easy it would be, I thought, to give up the fight, to become demoralised by the harsh environment. I did in fact meet people who seemed to have done this, who must have had many personal problems; and in contrast to most of the moorland kitchens, some I went into I could only describe politely as 'rough'. But without exception, people treated Cliff and myself with unfailing courtesy and good humour. I hope we treated them likewise. For me it was a great pleasure to meet them, for such people were a goldmine of information, as they had not modernised their

houses for generations. They still had bakestones in their kitchens and they made me feel that the old traditional ways were very close.

For most people in the nineteenth century, living further south in the area known as the Potteries was no piece of cake either. Domestic life in the mean houses and back yards must have required endurance to an extent we can scarcely imagine today. One of its saving graces no doubt was a strong sense of shared identity. With the ceramic industry so dependent on female labour, the skilled women of the potbanks must have found a fast, nourishing food like oatcakes, cheap and available ready-made from an old woman round the corner, a godsend.

But how were these two landscapes, moorland and urban, so different in appearance, linked by a common food? Addressing that question became the theme of my search.

TWO

A special food
An introduction to the Staffordshire oatcake

PLACE YOURSELF IN JANUARY 2008, 9 o'clock on a cold, damp and windy Sunday morning in Waterloo Street, Hanley, Staffordshire. Despite the time of day, you see a straggling queue of maybe half a dozen people, mostly men, one with a child balancing precariously on a scooter, others carelessly chatting in the middle of the road, all waiting patiently around a serving hatch which obviously started life as the front-room window of an ordinary terraced house. The hatch sports a blue awning, and on the sill is a board painted with the name 'Hole in the Wall (Oatcakes) oatcakes. org'. Trade is brisk, the chat good-humoured. Despite the cheerfulness, though, the customers are anxious to get away, for Sunday breakfast and Sunday newspapers call.

The Hole in the Wall is one of the oldest surviving oatcake-maker's shops in the Potteries, founded in the 1920s in the front room of a private terraced house. At the time of writing it is still a thriving little business, selling perhaps 800 dozen oatcakes a week (depending on the season) and the means of livelihood for several people. But its days may be numbered, for in the first few months of 2008 it became famous as the focus of a campaign to preserve building and business from demolition and urban renewal.[2] The passion, even filtered through the columns of the local paper, was real.

Eating oatcake is still a living tradition in the Staffordshire Potteries and amazingly the habit is spreading. Larger and softer than the better-known Scottish oatcake, Staffordshire oatcakes are similar to the soft oatcakes found in neighbouring counties, but the Staffordshire version seems to have gone deep into the soul of the area and to have survived more successfully than other variations. A generation or so ago, the traditional way to eat them was to warm them between two plates in an oven and serve them as an accompaniment to bacon and eggs for breakfast; or, more recently, sprinkled with cheese and simply toasted under a grill, then rolled. (Modern oatcake-makers note, please, the traditional recipe for Staffordshire cheese was very like Cheshire, not Cheddar.)[3] Over the last few years, however, oatcakes have taken on a new lease of life. Growing interest in healthy, fibre-rich foods, the increasing popularity of takeaways, and the ever-widening choice of exotic breads have resulted in the inclusion of oatcakes in the menus of cafes, restaurants and bars, posh golf clubs and genteel teashops. They are served in a variety of ways – including traditional, wrapped around curry, with smoked salmon and cream cheese, or with raspberry jam, whipped double cream, strawberries and icing sugar.[4] As at August 2008 there are well over 40 retail and wholesale oatcake-makers in North Staffordshire (p.116) and Staffordshire oatcakes can be bought in supermarkets not only in the county but also in other counties, London and major cities. Oatcakes have even adapted to the internet. Several makers have websites on which you can order takeaway oatcakes, plain ones to be delivered by first-class post, or filled ones, packed in microwaveable containers, to be delivered by courier. At my last excursion on the internet I found 13,000 'hits' for 'Staffordshire Oatcakes'.

Most of these were enquiries from 'ex-patriots' – exiles abroad. According to their website, the shop called Povey's Oatcakes in Biddulph has a regular order for eight dozen a month for Barclays Bank in Japan, and there is at least one ex-Kidsgrove man in Western Australia who has modified his barbecue so he can make up to seven oatcakes at a time![5] There is a commercial oatcake-maker in business in Benidorm and even the Staffordshire Regiment in Iraq was known to await with anticipation the occasional soldier flying out to join the regiment, bearing a load of oatcakes. Clearly something meaningful is going on.

Staffordshire oatcakes have been given the accolade of inclusion in the European Union's list of traditional regional foods. Probably few Potteries people – either oatcake-eaters or -makers – were aware of the existence of 'Euroterroirs', an initiative funded by the EU and given the task in the 1990s of identifying and describing traditional foods with a regional association.[6] The criteria for acceptance in the descriptions, which were published in 1995–6, were strict, but Staffordshire oatcakes clearly met all the requirements:

- Foods had to be linked to a region with the local name included in the name of the product.
- They had to have a proven history stretching over 3 generations or more (a generation was 25 years).
- They had to require 'savoir-faire', that is a specific knowledge of ingredients and methods of making.
- They should still be 'alive', ie regularly marketed.

By luck, I happened to know the compiler of the British list, Laura Mason, an eminent food historian. I pointed out to her the case of Staffordshire oatcakes and they were included in the published inventory, albeit the description, when finally published in English, proved slightly inaccurate. The idea behind the initiative was one of protection and recognition – certain foods are special to a region. More recently a more select list has been established by the EU of foods which are given the status of 'protected designation of origin'. Such foods are the cultural property of communities who have rights over them. Staffordshire oatcakes are not on this list.

Pottery people have always taken oatcakes for granted, but are aware that until recently others found them eccentric in their addiction. Perhaps oatcakes have always been the butt of jokes, although the humour is affectionate and protective and in itself speaks volumes for the place they hold in the society. There are many myths and prejudices and a surprising degree of variation between commercial makers – thick or thin, brown or golden, smooth or ragged, soft or crispy at the edges, sweetish or sharper in flavour. Some are slightly larger, thicker and softer than others and these tend to be the traditional handmade ones. Everyone has their favourite version and their favourite shop. People will travel miles to buy their oatcakes from a particular maker. Periodically the local newspaper and radio have indulged in a tongue-in-cheek discussion of the pros and cons and who has the best 'secret' recipe. When shops changed hands the recipe was usually sold with it and in the late twentieth century this could be valued at £1,000. Journalists often seem to refer to oatcakes as 'delicacies'; yet they are hardly a 'delicate' dish; rather they have a succulent robust presence reminiscent of a peasant food.

It might seem strange, therefore, that local Staffordshire historians have ignored oatcakes. Virtually none of the written local histories of the area even mention them. John Walton, in preparing his book on the history of fish and chips, found exactly the same problem:

> Fish and chips is generally recognised as a great and quintessentially British institution: but it is difficult to persuade people to take it seriously as a subject of historical enquiry ... it is held to be investing something trivial and risible with ludicrously inflated importance.[7]

It is almost as if the social stigma attached to a street food is transferred to the process of searching for its past.

So, where does it all come from and how unique are Staffordshire oatcakes? Many traditional foods are associated with myths which have grown up to explain them – such as the story that Bakewell pudding was first made by a servant who misunderstood her mistress's instructions. A modern myth, which I originally thought was just a joke, says the idea of oatcakes was brought back by the Staffordshire Regiment from service in the Indian Raj. This belief seems to be so common that refuting it is one of the reasons for writing this booklet. An older myth around the Potteries was that oatcakes were invented by people who took thin gruel to work for their breakfast and heated it on a stoker's shovel so that it solidified into cake. Such myths are interesting as social commentary or jokes, but, if seriously believed, they do an injustice to the true antiquity of our traditions.

Today, Staffordshire oatcakes may be a unique urban survival, but their origin lies deep in the history of rural Northern England and even of Europe. By the early Middle Ages, historians think the continent was divided roughly into three bread-eating areas on the basis of climate: the wheat-eating south; the rye-eating north; the oats- and barley-eating Atlantic fringe. Over time, in most European countries, those who could afford to do so preferred to eat bread made of wheat or of mixed grains – usually rye with wheat. This makes

The Hole in the Wall. Top: Sunday morning at the 'Hole in the Wall' oatcake shop, Waterloo Street, Hanley, which became the subject of a campaign to 'Save our Oatcakes' early in 2008. Centre: John and Miriam Clarkson, who bought The Hole in the Wall in 1963 and ran it for 20 years (Peter Clarkson). Bottom: Founded in the 1920s, in 2008 the shop was owned by Glenn Fowler who bought it in 1983

better bread than rye alone; only Prussia ate pure rye bread regularly. Lowland England was placed in the original rye belt but we too developed a preference for rye mixed with wheat. But because of high rainfall and short growing seasons, our northern and Atlantic fringes ate barley and oats. This is the origin of our oatcakes.

You can still buy soft oatcakes from a few market stalls and shops in Derbyshire, Lancashire and north-west Cheshire, made from basically similar recipes to the Staffordshire version, but slightly thicker or larger. Other variants of the old oatcake tradition of the north of England have also evolved and survived, such as the 'oven cakes', once called 'oven-bottom cakes', which are still available today from bakeries in Yorkshire.[8] These represent a stage in the development of oatcakes in which wheat flour gradually replaced oatmeal to create a kneaded cake cooked on the solid bottom of an oven. But the scale of the survival of a commercial trade in the true oatmeal-based oatcake of the Potteries and adjacent towns is unique, and the oatcake-eating habit goes deeper into the working-class culture of the Potteries than elsewhere. Why should this be? Why have they survived here? How have they changed? What do they tell us about our food in the past? Where did they originally come from? In a more general sense, do oatcakes as a feature of a cultural past reveal anything about the nature of change in our society?

We live at a time of rapid transitions in food tastes and supplies. In past centuries developments in the character or spread of foods were much slower. Historians of food innovation have recognised two different directions of travel of food changes: newly introduced foods which start as expensive luxuries at the top of the social hierarchy and spread downwards (one such example is tea); and foods which begin as famine foods, become a staple for lower social levels and gradually move upwards (one example being the potato).[9] Oats as a food source have changed the shape of their contribution to our diet following this second trajectory, moving from famine food to a high-status health food. The German food ethnologist Günther Wiegelmann was clear that oats were a famine food in Europe at a very early period and came to be accepted as a general food only very slowly.[10] On a much more local scale, Staffordshire oatcakes have changed from the basic staple of a relatively poor rural society to the treat food of a relatively rich urban one.

In order to tease out the details of this transition we must go back to the rural tradition. This has been described in several contemporary accounts and can be confirmed by evidence from inventories attached to wills, surviving objects and recorded memories. We can then go on to consider how and why this rural tradition came to flourish in the urban villages of the Potteries. Did it survive *in situ* the industrialisation of a previously rural way of life, changing as it did so; or was it grafted on afterwards, from the outside, permeating an existing working-class urban culture?

Unfortunately, nineteenth-century records of the urban tradition are extremely scarce, which in itself may tell us something about the position in society of both the food and its makers. The first commercial oatcake-makers usually operated on a level below official documentation. It is not until the early decades of the twentieth century that we can begin to see the details of an already established industrial tradition, using oral history as our major source of information.

THREE

'Avena sativa'

The origins, nature and advantages of oats

OATS HAVE MANY SPECIAL QUALITIES. Like rye, primitive oats were a weed amongst other cereals such as wheat and, as with most other early agricultural innovations, their cultivation probably originated in the Middle East. Cultivated versions appeared in Europe as early as the Bronze Age and though internet wisdom has it that it was the Romans who introduced oats to Britain, via German merchants trading between the Middle East and Roman Britain, oats have been identified by archaeologists in earlier pre-Roman sites in various areas of Britain. Evidence from carbonised grain and pollen comes from Bronze Age Cornwall, Iron Age Hampshire and the broch-dwellers of Scatness on Shetland whose diet included barley, oats, pork, veal, venison and milk.[11] The precise dating of the start of cultivation of oats in this country is obscure, though, because of the difficulty of distinguishing cultivated oats from wild.

Modern health-diet gurus have labelled oats as 'a true SuperFood'.[12] They have the highest protein content of all the cereals, so they form a good staple for a hard-working peasant or industrial society. However, they are low in calories but high in fibre content. Wholegrain oats contain beta-glucan, a polymer which makes soluble fibre which helps lower cholesterol and stimulates

www.wiganman.co.uk.

the immune system. Oats also contain avenan-thramides – an antioxidant compound which helps prevent the build-up of plaque on artery walls as well as stimulating the production of antihistamine. Modern studies have shown that a bowlful of porridge a day can reduce high cholesterol levels by between 8 and 23%, thus reducing the risk of heart disease, stroke and diabetes.[13] Not surprisingly, the consumption of oats in the United Kingdom is rising. Moreover, in 1990, the proportion of oats eaten as human food as opposed to livestock feed was far higher in the UK (44%) than in any other European country, outstripped only by Brazil, China and the Democratic Peoples Republic of Korea.[14]

Today we may know more about why oats are good for us, but the health-giving qualities of oats for a working population were also expounded by the dietary experts of generations ago. *The Lancet* commissioned a report in the mid-nineteenth century:

Oatmeal is an important and valuable article of food. With the exception of maize or Indian corn, it is richer in oily or fatty matter than any other of the cultivated cereal grains, and its proportion of protein compounds exceeds that of the finest English wheat–flour. So that both with respect to its heat-and-fat making, and its flesh-and-blood making principles, it holds a high rank.[15]

Oats contain a different combination of proteins to other cereals, and one which is reduced in oats relative to other cereals is gluten. This is important historically because gluten is an essential ingredient in 'normal' bread – gluten enables the bread to set in the presence of yeast. So oats were used in bread-making only in small amounts mixed with other bread-making cereals such as wheat and rye. A low-grade bread useful in times of food shortage, for example, was dredge, a mixture of barley and oats. The first successful solo use of oats, therefore, was almost certainly as a porridge-type gruel with water or milk, where the low gluten was unimportant.

Oatmeal, however, makes good flatbread. The Mexican *tortilla*, the Indian *chapati* and the Chinese *pao ping* are all survivors of a primitive form of unleavened flatbread which was easily made by mixing a cereal dough and spreading it on a flattish stone heated on top of a fire.[16] No complicated, expensive equipment

Oats and gluten

Although oats are lower in gluten than other cereals, they still have avenin, which can trigger a reaction in coeliacs and they are often contaminated by being processed alongside wheat. The Original Oaties Company in Dresden, Staffordshire, make an 'oatcake' mix suitable for sufferers from coeliac disease. Wheat-flour and oatmeal are replaced by rice, tapioca, potato, sarrasin and carob, but the taste and texture has been retained.

(You can also buy gluten-free oatcakes at Weston Coyney Oatcakes, www.westoncoyneyoatcakes.co.uk)

such as an oven was needed. Early evidence of such hearth-cakes comes from a first-century BC lake-village site at Glastonbury, where the unleavened cakes were made of whole grains of wheat, barley and wild oats.[17] Such early cakes seem to have been of a dough-like consistency, but oatcakes in general relate to a venerable international family of foods – early independent responses to similar circumstances.

Of greater importance historically than all the health qualities is the fact that, in the ground, oats are tolerant of poor weather conditions. They can survive higher rainfall, a shorter growing season and later spring frosts than barley, wheat or rye. They can be harvested later than other cereals. A diary written in the 1780s by a land agent living at Pilsbury on the Staffordshire/Derbyshire border recorded starting the oat harvest on October 6th, which he regarded as

Milling oats

'Six hundredweights at a time, spread about six inches deep, were dried for five hours in the kiln heated with furnace coke. Turned with a wooden shovel by a miller wearing clogs or boots with thick soles, the oats were heated until too hot to hold, when they were ready. They then went twice through a pair of Derbyshire Peak stones, the first for shelling and the second for grinding and lastly through six layers of wire mesh riddles. The products were mill dust which fell through the riddles, the groats, used for havermeal, and the husks ... which weighing light were sent to Liverpool in large sacks for packing pottery to send abroad.'

(M. Hartley and J. Ingilby, *Life and Tradition in the Yorkshire Dales*, 1968, p. 26)

very early.[18] Oats could be left stooked in the field to dry out for longer than other grains and often were not harvested until into November. This is not to say that oats do not prefer better conditions; farmers in Hollinsclough have told me that when they grew oats in the old days it was only one year in four or five

Oat straw was highly valued as the favourite bedding for cattle, horses and humans (in straw-stuffed palliases), as it is relatively soft, dust-free and absorbent. Its flexibility made it the preferred straw for stuffing collars for working horses. It made good 'feedstraw' too – livestock would eat the leaves left on the straw if hay was scarce.

which was dry enough to give a really good hard-grained crop which would mill well. A wet summer would produce soft-grained oats, difficult to mill but still easy to 'roll' or flatten using large stones. So oats can survive poor weather and still provide a reasonable yield. It was this toughness which gave them a place in the medieval three-field system of crop rotation; if all else failed, there would be oatmeal of some sort to stave off famine. They became part of the tradition of 'allowancing' – paying part of the annual wages of farm labourers in meal or grain.[19] This system was critical to the rural diet for centuries and lasted longer in the north of England than the south. From Wales, too, there is evidence that oats were used instead of cash in the payment of tithes in the Middle Ages and as donations to the poor.[20] Flat oatbread had the added advantage of not needing to be cooked in a manorial oven, which could be expensive.

Rolled oats are ideally suited as a livestock feed. They were the best food for horses and thus grew in importance with the increase of horse-drawn transport and the change from oxen to horses as farm draught animals. It has even been claimed that oats contributed to the socialisation of rural communities – they enabled the feeding of more horses for riding and carting, and thus men became more mobile and more gregarious.[21]

Studies of medieval food in England using monastic and household accounts show the ubiquity of 'potage' for working people. This was a gruel usually based on oatmeal with peas and beans, though ingredients varied widely according to what was available.[22] Even in southern England, oatmeal was a favourite thickening agent for potage; but there, oats were not used as breadcorn because better alternatives were available and a host of different qualities of bread was made, perhaps the commonest being maslin bread, made from a mixture of rye and wheat. In the colder, wetter north, oats were all they had for everyday use, so they became even more important in different ways – various forms of flat-bread, hard and soft, as well as potage. This was true of many parts of Wales, too, where oatcakes were a staple food throughout the medieval period and later.[23]

Where and when the idea of making flatbread from oats originated within the British Isles is unknown. It seems clear that Iron Age people had oats but did they use them in some sort of bread or just in potage – the origin of our porridge? Certainly Pliny reported that the Germanic tribes of that period grew oats and used them as a staple in the form of porridge.[24] One modern writer places the use of oats in flatbread in Saxon times and another ascribes them to 'the 12th century at least'.[25] Certainly the word 'bakestone', the equipment closely associated with oatcakes, is of Old English origin. Another possible clue may be the Northern name given to some types of oatcake – havercake – from the Old Norse word for oats. Do we owe the idea of oatcake, as opposed to oats in potage, to the settlers from Europe who came after the Roman withdrawal? Or were they even older?

The miracle food

If one-quarter of the claims made for oats are true, we should all be living off them all the time!

Eating oats will:

1. Boost your sex life
2. Cure a hangover
3. Help you stop smoking
4. Heal the skin
5. Fight infection
6. Fight heart disease
7. Reduce risk of diabetes
8. Help concentration
9. Beat depression and S.A.D.
10. Provide a boost to energy levels
11. Cut childhood obesity
12. Lower cholesterol
13. Prevent constipation
14. Fight osteoporosis
15. Help dieting
16. Help pregnant women
17. Fight cancer
18. Contain essential minerals
19. Reduce blood pressure
20. Help ensure a long life

Did you know oats were responsible for the invention of the bicycle!?

In 1816, the eruption of Mount Tambora in Indonesia resulted in a worldwide volcanic winter and a summer which never was. The price of oats rocketed, resulting in the starvation of many horses and hence many transport problems. This is turn led Baron Karl von Drais of Mannheim to experiment with an invention called a dandy horse – the direct precursor of the bicycle.

(Angela Epstein, *Oat Cuisine*, www.dailymail.co.uk, April, 2008)

Even in the 1950s oats were a safe crop to grow. They grew tall and often fell flat or 'necked over'. But that was not a problem – they could still be combined easily.

Oats as a fuel for farm workers

Early in the twentieth century, the labourers on a farm at Bucknall, right in the centre of the Potteries, would come in from their early morning work in the fields to 'fill-belly' – a stiff oat porridge which was put to cool and solidify in a special wooden 'drawer'. The workers would cut off slices for themselves.

(Thanks to Keele WI)

Oatcake warnings!

'Indulgence leads to Bulgence' (Arthur Berry)

Many oral and written memories of oatcakes recall scraping the fur off the mouldy bits. This seems to have had no bad effect, but oats, especially wild oats, can be a host for *Claviceps purpurea*, a fungus which causes the hallucinations, convulsions and gangrene associated with ergotism. This form of poisoning has been well documented from the Middle Ages, though it was more usually associated with rye than oats; but a case as recent as 1978 in Ethiopia has been traced back to barley contaminated with ergotised wild oats. The ergot fungus appears not as green mould but as dark bits very similar to rat droppings. Nevertheless it seems as well not to eat mouldy oatcakes!

FOUR

Havercake, riddlebread and sour oatcakes
The wider Pennine horizon

S TAFFORDSHIRE OATCAKES ARE PART OF A WIDER TRADITION of flat oatbread-making and eating which has been well-recorded from parts of the Pennines and it is important to point out this wider context.[26] Today it is difficult to imagine cereal-growing in the Pennines, but as Speight pointed out with reference to Nidderdale:

> There was a time when nearly every rood of land on the hillsides … was ploughed and sown almost wholly with oats, garnered and consumed in the district.[27]

Opposite: a domestic oatcake-maker depicted in 1814. Although this watercolour shows a Yorkshire kitchen, many of the fittings would have been similar to those of a Pennine farmhouse in Staffordshire. Behind the woman is a built-in bakestone, on the stool is a deep 'panchion' or 'jowl' for mixing the pouring dough, in the front a chair is used as a cooling rack – all of which figure in Staffordshire moorland memories. (George Walker, 'Costume of Yorkshire', 1814)

Speight went on to explain that the farmers practised contour ploughing – moving across the hillsides not up and down them – to reduce runoff and soil erosion. This was much easier with oxen or horse ploughs than with modern machines, which tend to tip over. The crop was needed not only for human food, of course, but also for animal feed, in a society when all long distance travel and haulage depended on horses.

The growing of oats in the Pennines has been well researched by historians and historical geographers in the past. Dudley Stamp defined the limits of commercially viable wheat cultivation as being the 60°F isotherm in July and below 30″ annual rainfall. Most of the Pennines fall outside the wheat-growing areas on both criteria. This wheat limit coincides closely with what historian William Kapelle called (in memory of Dr Johnson!) the 'oatbread line', which defined that part of the north of England where oats and barley were more important than wheat and rye.[28] This formed a fundamental division of northern England until the mid-eighteenth century, when the beginnings of modern transport networks began to break the link between diet and local agriculture. It does not mean that wheat could never be grown in these areas, but it would flourish only in very sheltered favoured spots and would never be wholly dependable. For the medieval peasant, of course, this was not good enough; for him, a failed crop meant starvation.

Working from Arthur Young's reports of his travels in northern England in the 1760s, Kapelle described several bread areas in the north. These areas do not delineate different cultures of bread-eating entirely, since the better-off people could afford to buy breadcorn out of the district, but they do reveal the cereals which did best within a given area. In summary, the plain to the east of the Pennines was generally a wheat-bread area, changing to rye-bread north of the Vale of York into Durham and southern Northumberland, and to bread made with barley mixed with ground peas further north. The eastern slopes of the Pennines in Yorkshire were a soft oatbread region, as also were the central and western Pennines and adjacent areas from Westmorland into Lancashire as far south as Cheshire and Staffordshire. Finally there was a zone running down the plain west of the Pennines from Cumbria as far south as Newcastle-under-Lyme in which the main bread corn was barley. To the north of England as a whole, of course, came the very different Scottish tradition of oatcake-eating in the form of hard biscuits.

These areas could still be broadly recognised in the early nineteenth century, when the government instituted the Board of Agriculture reports on the farming practices of each English county. But Kapelle maintained that the 'oatbread line' was much older, having cut across the North since prehistoric times, though with fluctuations with changes in climate, taste

Thrown oatcakes being made by Mr Wells of Skipton. In 1960 he was the only remaining commercial maker of this form of oatcake. Though the old domestic makers threw the batter onto the bakestone by hand, Mr Wells used a degree of automation. At the far end by the wall is a home-made 'trolley' which was rolled very sharply over the bakestone, thus throwing the batter into the characteristic oval shape.
(Beamish Museum. Photograph Frank Atkinson)

and farm practices. It has certainly been confirmed in Lancashire in the thirteen century and there is some evidence for the existence of a barley-bread tradition north-west of Newcastle-under-Lyme.[29]

For Kapelle the 'oatbread line' was important not in itself but in relation to the Norman settlement of northern England. The Normans came to England for land but they were habitual wheat-bread eaters and regarded oatbread as a strange, low, peasant food. They therefore tended to avoid settling on estates 'beyond the oatbread line' as this gave them low status amongst their peers. It is interesting that this Norman characterisation of oatbread as being low status has lasted for so many centuries and has only recently been eroded.

In the Yorkshire Pennines, several different kinds of oatbread were recorded as early as 1674.[30] The varieties were of two basic types: one made from a stiff dough called variously havercake, clapbread (from the old tradition of 'clapping' it out into shape between the hands); and the second made with a thinner pouring dough. This latter usually contained barm (liquid yeast usually taken from the brewer) or was 'soured' by mixing in leftover dough from the previous making. These poured oatcakes were called variously riddlebread, oatcake and sometimes 'kitcheness' bread.[31] Riddlebread was often the name given to a thrown version of the poured type cake. In this the batter was poured onto a wooden 'riddleboard' which was usually scored with a diamond pattern and seasoned with dry oatmeal; board and batter were then gently shaken in a circular movement to make a neat shape of batter, which was then slid onto the hot bakestone top to cook. Sometimes the batter was transferred from the riddleboard onto yet another board covered with a piece of fine linen; from this the batter was literally thrown sideways onto the bakestone, resulting in a characteristic oval shape rather than a circle. A good description of this method was written by Frank Atkinson in 1960, by Moody in an article on Yorkshire dialect published in 1997, and in a booklet entitled *Making Oatcake*, published in 1998 in the West Riding.[32] This tradition of thrown oatcake seems to have been dying out in parts of Yorkshire in the mid-nineteenth century.[33] A simpler method of making oval cakes was to spoon the batter on to the bakestone in a strip rather than a circle.

Within these two general types there existed a great variety of Pennine and Cumbrian oatcakes, with many local names. These have been identified and their geographical and dialect complexities worked out by researchers such as Marie Hartley and Frank Atkinson.[34] Although the details of recipes and methods vary, they have many basic features in common, not least some of the names given to equipment. A similar tradition, mainly of dough-type oatcakes, has been recorded in detail from Wales.[35] The Staffordshire and Derbyshire oatcakes seem always to have been of the thin-batter, pouring, non-throwing type. I have never found a Staffordshire reference to oval oatcakes or to dough-type cakes.

So what was the tradition in the south Pennine moorlands of Staffordshire and Derbyshire? Here climate and geology conspired to offer the farmer only poor soils and a short growing season, making the cultivation of wheat impossible, and barley difficult. In 1686, Robert Plot recognised this:

> The black, Moorish and gouty grounds of the Moorlands with the best helps are fit indeed only for oats and barley.[36]

Oats were still the pre-eminent cereal in the area over a century later at the beginning of the nineteenth century. A summary of the Crop Returns for 1801 – a sort of cereal census taken by the Secretary of State concerned about the Napoleonic War – shows the acreages of cereals produced by each parish. In the Staffordshire moorland parish of Butterton the only cereal acreage was oats – no wheat or barley at all – and Alstonefield, Calton, Meerbrook, Onecote, Sheen and Wetton each had less than 10 acres down to wheat or barley, compared

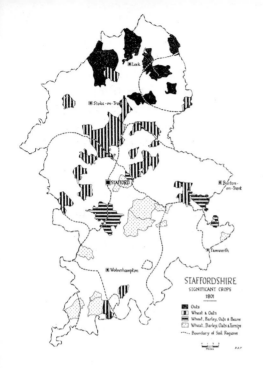

Map showing the significant crop acreages in Staffordshire in 1801. (R. A. Pelham. The 1801 Crop Returns for Staffordshire in their geographical setting, *Collections for a History of Staffordshire*, 1950–51, pp. 231–42)

with a total of over 1,400 acres of oats.[37] The map of significant crop acreages in Staffordshire was compiled by R. A. Pelham from the same data and shows the supremacy of oats in the moorland area. Notice, however, that oats were also grown alongside the less hardy cereals in other arable parts of the county.

In the absence of other local authorities at the time, the 1801 Crop Returns were compiled by vicars and collected by the Bishop of each diocese. Pelham writes:

The Curate of Meerbrook in the Parish of Leek felt compelled to observe that his district had a 'late, cold Climate; & by consequence but ill calculated by Nature for the production of Grain excepting Oats; and those indeed of an inferior Sort, being chiefly black ones' … The Vicar of nearby Biddulph comments to the effect that 'the daily bread of the Inhabitants is Oat Cake'[38]

Strictly speaking, subsistence agriculture, that is reliance on home-grown foodstuffs, had ceased by the eighteenth century, by which time there was a growing trade in meal. But by then conservative habits were ingrained and the old custom of eating oats as a staple form of bread persisted. Thus our oatcakes are a remnant of a food system which dates from before the de-localisation of our food supply.

Important though it was to the moorlanders, outsiders tended to regard oatcake with disdain – it was still regarded as a low level subsistence food. We can see this amongst most of the writers of general, social and agricultural accounts of the area in the eighteenth and nineteenth centuries, who visited the area from outside. Thomas Brown, for example, travelled the moorland areas at the end of the eighteenth century to report on the agriculture of Derbyshire:

> Travelling farther north in the High Peak, we find hardly anything like a regular rotation of crops. The quantity of land under tillage is comparatively nothing; oats, oats, oats (and, alas, sour oatcakes) a few potatoes, a little barley, and still less wheat would be the food of the natives did not their neighbours cultivate their land better than they do. Their mutton, however, is excellent.[39]

In contrast, William Pitt, the writer of a companion report on Staffordshire, seems to have identified with the natives of the moorlands a little more sympathetically:

> The country not being populous, and oat-bread in general use, the demand for wheat is not very great ... Oatbread is eaten very generally in the Moorlands, and none other is kept in the country houses; this however, I cannot consider as any criterion of poverty, or of a backward or unimproved state, as I think it

equally wholesome, palatable and nutritive as wheat bread, and little cheaper even here; for upon enquiry in Leek I found oatmeal and wheat flour nearly the same price. For several days during my stay in this country, I ate no other bread from choice, preferring it to other bread, and rather wonder it is not more general and kept in London and elsewhere for such palates as prefer it. In remote country villages it is often baked thick with sour leven, and a proportion of oat husks; this, even when ground mouldy, is eaten by the natives without murmuring.[40]

We have a more detailed account of oatbread and its manufacture on a large farm at Pilsbury Grange, near Hartington, on the Staffordshire/Derbyshire border, written by another agriculturalist, William Farey, in 1813:[41]

Instead of using Yeast or Barm in the making of Haver-cake, as is very general in some part of Yorkshire, an acid fermentation is excited in the Leaven or Batter, of which the Derbyshire Cakes are made, by a sour wooden Tub called a Doshen, in which it is mixed; and during the winter months, the House-wives are very careful not to wash out the Doshen or tub, in which the Batter is mixed and fermented, but to leave a little of the Batter each time adhering to its sides, to commence the fermentation of the next batch; in summer time the Doshen is slightly washed out with cold water after each baking, the tub itself being then sufficiently sour to raise the next leaven. At Mr Joseph Gould's at Pilsbury, I saw the process of baking for his farm-servants ... The Batter, something thicker than that which is used for Pancakes, is poured onto the bakestone, (here a cast-iron plate, with a fire under it) from a wooden Dish, and is spread by the back of a wooden ladle

The hamlet of Pilsbury and the Goulds' farm where William Farey recorded the process of oatcake-making in 1813. Top right is the building at the back which is now a separate house but which once accommodated the farm workers and the kitchen where Farey watched the oatcakes being made.

to about one-fourth of an inch thick, and 16 or 18 inches diameter: a cake-slice or long thin iron spatula is short after used, to run under the Cake, to release it from the stone, and if the back part of the stone is less or more hot than the front, it is turned round by the slice: after it has been about 1¼ to 1½ minutes on the stone, the edges are raised by the slice, and the point of a thin wooden bake-spittle, or cake-board, is dexterously shoved under the Cake, and it is turned over and thrown again on the stone, and if necessary, is smoothed by the slice; about 2½ to 2¾ minutes after, it is turned again, and about 2½ to 2¾ minutes more, having been released and turned round if necessary as in the interval before, it is taken off by the spittle, and laid hollow across the earthen pan, considerably smaller than the Cake, to steam, for a few minutes; and when

another Cake is each ready, it is removed to a pile upon a board, in close contact with other, which pile of Cakes is removed to a dry cool place, not too airy, for use during the three to seven following days, according as they bake once or twice in the week. The flat bakestones are used in many parts of the County, instead of an iron plate, and are thought to make lighter and better cake, and which will keep longer; but all the operations are nearly twice as long as above, in performing, and the consumption of fuel consequently much greater. A greasy linen rag, is rubbed over the stone or plate between every three or more cakes, to prevent their burning, but sometimes this need not be repeated oftener than every tenth Cake. At Mr. Ellis Needham's Cotton-mill Apprentice-house in Litton, soured oatcakes … are used one day old in summer, and two days old in winter.

This account gives us a number of objects and characteristics to bear in mind when looking for other sources, the most important of which have proved to be probate inventories attached to wills. But before moving on to these searches we need a little more explanation about bakestones.

FIVE

Bakestones and griddles
From c.200AD to c.2000AD

Bakestones (called 'girdles' or 'griddles' in the midlands and the north of England) were not limited to oatcake-cooking or to oatcake regions, as they were used for cooking a variety of scones and flat cakes. But they were a universal piece of equipment in the Pennine hill regions where they were used primarily for flat oatcake. The name bakestone is Old English in origin – 'baec-stan', meaning 'a flat stone for baking on'. The name is first recorded from the twelfth century and according to English place-name evidence has a marked northern distribution.[42] The original bakestones were of stone, but our grandmothers used the same word for a flat metal plate and even modern oatcake-makers in the Potteries have retained it for their large gas-fired hotplates.

In Wales stone bakestones were made of slate but in the Pennines they were usually of a fine-grained shaley sedimentary rock in the millstone grit series, usually coloured greyish pink.[43] This level of grit has obviously good cleavage – it splits like slate. Large pieces weighing several hundredweights were quarried from rock outcrops at the sides of steep valleys and carried from the pit on the back of a man. Once quarried the stone becomes very friable and breaks up easily. For this reason, the large pieces were split up by men working at the side of a stream where the slices of rock could be kept immersed in water to protect and 'temper' them. Here they were also worked into a smooth shape of the required size, using an old scythe blade. They were then fired in a pit to harden them.[44]

Much of the earliest evidence for the existence of bakestones and quarries comes from local place-names. In the Pennines, many names testify to sites where such fine flaggy sandstones were dug out for the purpose. Those in northern England have been mapped by Angus Winchester.[45] David Horovitz in his work on Staffordshire placenames also found several examples, including 'Baxstonehurst' near Whitmore and 'Bacstonesley' – from the Elkstone region, dated 1332.[46] Another example is Bakestonedale, near Pott Shrigley on the Cheshire edge of the moorlands.[47] The name of Baxenden in Lancashire also derives from quarrying bakestones. The most important quarry, however, was further north, at Delph near Saddleworth, from where there is a record of 'William and Robert Bakestoman' in 1330.[48]

Circular or a rounded square and flat, up to two inches thick and twenty-four inches across, stone bakestones were either supported in front of the fire on an iron framework, a sort of trivet, or suspended on an iron framework fitted with a looped handle to hang over the fire from a chimney 'crane'. These frameworks were called variously 'brand irons' or more accurately 'bearers'. Examples of stone bakestones have survived in museums, especially the Saddleworth Museum, near Oldham. In the early nineteenth century Farey described stone bakestones as being commonly used in cottages on a hanging trivet.[49]

Quarrying and cutting stone bakestones was a skilled job involving hand-crafting and exposure to all weathers. Men could make a good living from it, selling the stones by hawking them around the towns and countryside in panniers

Left: James Mill, bakestone maker at work beside Hull Brook, Saddleworth, *c.* 1910. Shaped stones are tempering in the stream. Right: James Mill and Arthur Schofield outside a hut inside which bakestones were fired to harden. (Saddleworth Museum Archives)

on ponies, or on market stalls.[50] It is a relatively well-documented trade from early times and there is indeed a record of the tolls charged for a horse-load of bakestones at Manchester market in 1320.[51]

During the seventeenth century the latest in kitchen luxury would have been not a stone bakestone but a cast iron one. Probate inventory evidence strongly implies an iron bakestone was present on a farm near Sheen, on the Staffordshire/Derbyshire border, in 1617 (see below), and there are records of iron bakestones being supplied on two farms in Yorkshire in 1656.[52] Iron bakestones may be much earlier in origin, however, as evidenced by an iron example excavated at a thirteenth-century cottage site at Beere in Devon, probably used for making wheat flatbread.[53] The earlier examples were simply circular flat iron plates, whilst the nineteenth-century versions incorporated their own iron loop, often made to fold down. These became very common throughout the nineteenth century, of course, as iron goods became more affordable.

The story of bakestones is much more complicated than this, however. Large farms with a substantial living-in work force to feed often had not circular bakestones but larger permanent fixed structures – flat rectangular plates of stone or cast iron perhaps three or four foot long, built over a firebox and ash pit and usually provided

In 1664 Bishop John Hacket of Lichfield visited Stanton Hall, birthplace of Archbishop Sheldon, where he was entertained with oatcakes and 'nappy' (i.e. strong) ale.

(A. G. Mathews, *Congregational Churches of Staffordshire*, 1924, p. 69)

with a vent or connection to the chimney. There is evidence of a fixed bakestone being built at Shibden Hall near Halifax from as early as 1684, possibly still a fixed stone slab rather than iron. Other evidence shows fixed iron plates being fitted in the West Riding of Yorkshire by 1814 and 'iron planks', which sound like fixed bakestones, appear in Welsh inventories from the seventeenth and eighteenth centuries.[54]

It is probable that the idea of a fixed, built-in bakestone, made of stone not iron, is much earlier, however, and the evidence, strangely enough, comes from Staffordshire, from a Romano-British village site at Wetton, excavated between 1848 and 1852 by a local amateur archaeologist, Samuel Carrington. The area he dug covered many house sites as well as a barrow, in a place known today as Borough Fields. So substantial was the site that Carrington called it 'the very Pompeii of North Staffordshire'.[55] Several skeletons were found along with grave goods and many broken domestic items of bone, iron, bronze and pottery, both coarse and 'highly finished ware exhibiting a Roman character'. There were several fragments of quern stones for grinding corn, also coins of Roman date (Emperor Gallienus, AD 253–268), so the Romano-British date seems possible, though we have to reserve judgement due to the early date of the excavation.[56] The excavator described a structure in one of the house sites as follows:

> … a low wall built of flat limestones, in which was inserted a hard slab of gritty slate, about an inch thick, that had evidently been used as a bakestone, as it projected out from the wall so as to receive the heat of a fire kindled beneath it, the traces of which were obvious both upon the stone itself and the ground beneath it, whereon lay a collection of ashes and charcoal.

This was the only mention of a stone wall in the original account of the excavation. John Ward, a later writer who included reference to the site in his book published in 1911, concluded that as the houses were mainly of timber construction with thatched roofs, the wall's only purpose was to carry the bakestone. If so, it was testament to the importance of the bakestone in the household economy.

Excavation techniques being what they were at the time, Carrington left no plan and no note of the survival of cereal grains. There was also, worryingly, a very rough two pronged fork amongst the finds – though the Romans did use forks of this type.

Fixed bakestones were obviously more expensive than the freestanding variety since they were built-in with fire box, flue and ash pit, either in their own arch in the kitchen next to the main cooking hearth, or in an outhouse, often next to a fixed laundry boiler or slop sink. They were always an expensive piece of equipment to run as well as to construct, as they needed a separate fire built specially for them, not using the general fire like the small individual bakestones. This must have been particularly relevant in the north of England in the sixteenth and seventeenth centuries when population growth resulted in a 'relentless quest for fuel' for domestic purposes, and strict limitations imposed on common rights of fuel gathering.[57]

Most early fixed iron bakestones were rectangular. In the nineteenth century, however,

A piece of weathered millstone grit from Combs Moss near Buxton, showing the thin layering exploited by the bakestone makers. The individual layers here are scarcely more than a centimetre thick.

Above: Borough Fields near Wetton, possibly a Romano-British site dated to around AD 200 and excavated by Samuel Carrington of Wetton in 1848. Right: sketch of how the bakestone excavated at Borough Fields might have looked, from Samuel Carrington's description. (Jim Sutton)

A fitted bakestone at Devonshire Arms Farm, Sheldon, photographed in 2007. The cooking surface was the old style – a slab of millstone grit. This kitchen has since been modernised and the bakestone removed. (Photograph by Sheila Hine, from 'Around the White Peak' by Sheila Hine with Claude Fearns, Churnet Valley Books, 2007, p. 101)

Right: fixed bakestones were common throughout the Pennines. They were still fairly numerous in Yorkshire in the late 1960s when researchers Marie Hartley and Joan Ingilby saw fourteen examples. This one was in a farmhouse in Dentdale, Yorkshire. The fireplace was dated to 1800. The bakestone was a rectangle of iron built over a firebox and ash pit. (From Hartley and Ingilby 'Making Oatcake', Smith Settle, 1998, p. 33)

Middle and bottom right: A fixed bakestone in a farmhouse in Hollinsclough, still in place in 2009. The house dates to at least 1603 and probably earlier. The top of the bakestone is made from two metal plates. (Photograph and information V. K. Rowe)

Bottom left: a modern commercial gas-fired 'backstun' in use in Biddulph today.

Opposite: A fixed bakestone in the kitchen of a farm at Upper Hulme. The cooking surface was a single slab of iron. The kitchen was modernised in the 1970s. Did the same stonemason make this and the one in Hollinsclough? Were there stonemasons who specialised in fitting kitchens? (Staffordshire Arts and Museum Service. Photograph Cliff Gutteridge)

Top right: A fixed bakestone in the kitchen of a farmhouse at Bottomhouses. In this case a circular iron griddle was built-in over its own fire box and ash hole next to the copper boiler and slop sink (to the right). The house has been modernised since the 1970s when this photograph was taken. (Staffordshire Arts and Museum Service. Photograph Cliff Guttridge)

Left and bottom: a fixed iron bakestone built next to a washing copper in the back kitchen of Over Boothlow Farm, near Longnor. Photographed in 1970, since when the house has been modernised (Staffordshire Arts and Museum Service)

fixed bakestones were built using circular plates, probably in fact normal free-standing bakestones simply fitted into the top surface (as at Bottomhouses and Over Boothlow). Within living memory, some large farms even had two fixed bakestones; Moody recorded a pair in a farm near Addingham in Yorkshire, which made oatcakes for sale. One of the bakestones was kept hotter than the other to cook the first side of the oatcake; after it was turned it was put onto the cooler stone.[58] Although in Addingham the oatcakes were of the oval thrown variety, exactly the same system for ordinary poured oatcakes using two fixed bakestones was described to me twenty years ago from Longnor.

The modern commercial oatcake-makers in the Potteries still call their stoves 'backstuns'. Today these are gas-fired. According to the Yorkshire historian Marie Hartley large commercial backstones were invented by Joseph Wright, an ironmaster from Shipley, Yorkshire, in the middle of the nineteenth century, though there is no record of a patent in the Patent Library in London.

They probably only became common in the Potteries in the 1930s.

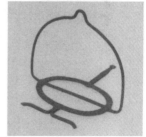

Top: iron bakestone or girdle with folding hanger. This example is flat but many iron bakestones were slightly domed to enable the mixture to settle into an even circle. The Scottish food historian F. Marian McNeill tells us that circular iron 'girdles' were first made in Culross, Fife, in the 1590s. (McNeill, *The Scots Kitchen*, 1929, p. 49)
Bottom: a hanging support for a bakestone.

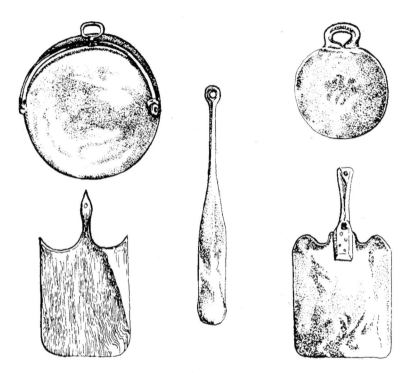

Top: Two types of small iron bakestone or griddle – one flat and one hanging – the latter with a handle which can be folded down.

Above centre: steel oatcake slice for loosening the oatcake as it cooks.

Below: Two oatcake sprittles – wooden (left) and metal with a wooden handle, for lifting the oatcake from the bakestone. Are wooden sprittles, older in origin than metal ones, the origin of the line in Arthur Berry's poem (p.iv) 'Or woodcake as the old men called them'?

Drawings not to scale

SIX

Baxtons, sprittles and arks
Inventory evidence about oatcake-making

BAKESTONES, whether iron or stone, have occasionally survived, but many of the tools used by the domestic oatcake-maker were of wood, made by the local carpenter or cooper, and were much more likely to have fallen apart or been damaged and thrown away over time. However, the presence of a rural oatbread-making habit similar to that described at Pilsbury is witnessed by primary manuscript sources from Staffordshire, which have preserved for us some of the dialect words for such tools. Inventories drawn up for the purposes of probate and attached to wills in the diocesan records of Lichfield survive for the period from the fifteenth to the mid-eighteenth centuries. They record the existence on specific farms of some of the oatbread-associated equipment described by Farey, itemised by specific names in the inventories such as bakestones, sprittles, slices, dashons and meal arks (these last were wooden, usually oak, chests used for storing oats and bacon).

Searching the wills and inventories was a tedious job as they were catalogued by date rather than place. I used several methods. Firstly, a friend of mine, Elspeth Walker, made a search of a very restricted area – around Sheen and Alstonefield, near Longnor. She turned up nine examples of wills and inventories from the sixteenth and seventeenth centuries, all showing evidence of oats. All have at least one 'arke', sometimes several; most have 'meale' and some also have 'oats'. One has a 'dosion' – the dough tub mentioned by Farey. There are three 'baxtons', the earliest from an inventory of Thomas Olyver dated 1557. Were these 'baxtons' stone or iron? The inventories are not clear on this point, but one dated 1617, from Whyttle Bank, lists the 'baxton' amongst other iron goods as follows: 'All other iron ware and harrows and one baxton 8s', which would indicate it was iron. Two other inventories list the 'baxton' completely separate from the iron items.

The nine inventories from Sheen and Alstonefield are:

1557 Thomas Olyver, Alstonefield

1587 John Bateman, Sheen

1606 William Horobin Sheen

1616 Thomas Percival, Sheen

1617 William Horobin, Whyttle Bank

1624 William Milward, Alstonfield

1630 Raphe Gilman, Sheen

1647 Henry Cocke, Hawksyard

1705 William Horobin, Sheen

Secondly, I looked at all the inventories from the county of Staffordshire in a single year, 1725. The results of this are shown on the map (p.48). Entries specifying oatbread equipment appear only from that area of the county north of Stone, and are limited entirely to farmers' inventories. So this gives us a

Extract from the will of Thomas Olyver, Alstonefield, 1557

In his will –	*I bequeathe to John my sonne An Arke*		
Inventory	*Item A payre of tonnges*	*iid*	[2d]
extract	*Item A brandeyrne*	*xiiiid*	[14d]
	Item A Axcell tre of lyrne to a grynle stone and the grindles	*xd*	[10d]
	Item iii Arkes and tornell	*xvid*	[16d]
	Item vi Ale lomes and a fate	*iiis*	[3s]
	Item A baxton	*vid*	[6d]
	Item A dosion and a chourne	*viiid*	[8d]
	Item A haroo and A Axe	*xiid*	[12d]
	Item iii bushel of ottes	*xxxs*	[30s]
	Item iii hopes of otte meyle	*xiis*	[12s]
	Summa totalis	*xixL vs viid*	
	[Total sum of whole inventory £19 5s 7d]		

(Original of the inventory extract)

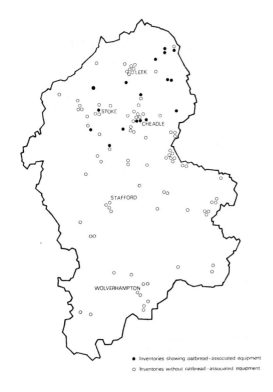

Oatbread-associated equipment in
Staffordshire from probate inventories in the
Lichfield Record Office for the year 1725.

● Inventories showing oatbread-associated equipment
○ Inventories without oatbread-associated equipment

clue to the geographical spread of oatcake-making in Staffordshire in the eighteenth century.

Thirdly, I searched all the inventories for the parish of Alstonefield in the period 1725 to 1740. Alstonefield is the most northerly parish of Staffordshire and covers a wide area of the moorlands including the villages of Grindon, Wetton, Warslow, Hulme End, Longnor and Hollinsclough. This more detailed search through the fifteen-year period from 1725 yielded a total of 83 wills for the Alstonefield parish, 45 of which contained either no inventory or only a cursory one. This left 38 detailed inventories of which all but six included oatcake-making or oat-storing items. Of these 32, seven recorded the presence of one or more bakestones, in five cases described as 'iron bakestones'. Two 'backstones' were listed with other iron cooking utensils, so it is probable that they too were iron and not stone.

Whether they were fixed or free-standing is not clear, although usually built-in immovable equipment was not included in probate inventories. However, individual valuations, where they exist, may be some guide: most valuations are around 1s, whereas Richard Bonsall's iron bakestone at Westside was valued at 5s in 1725, and this was possibly a fixed type since the remains of an old brick-built, iron-topped bakestone were left in the kitchen at Westside until the twentieth century. Visiting Westside Farm today and seeing the size of the old barn brings home the fact that many of these farms, though working on the fringes of cultivable land, did include rich pasturage along the valley bottoms (see p.59). The larger farms were important suppliers of milk, butter and cheese, and their hay and fodder storage capacity suggests a fair-sized livestock herd and thus a sizeable number of farm servants – all requiring feeding.

Turning to other pieces of equipment in the inventories of Alstonefield, 'back' or 'bake sprittles' were mentioned in five inventories, slices in four. 'Dashons' or 'daucions', the wooden tub mentioned by Farey, figured in seven inventories, usually in association with other wooden tubs such as churns, bouks, (wooden buckets), piggins (small containers) and gawns (gallon-sized). The written word appears in the inventories in a number of forms: 'dashion', 'dashon', 'dasheon' and 'daucion'. The word does not appear in printed Staffordshire dialect sources.[59] Only two 'dashons' were valued individually, as 3s and 1s. Amongst the Alstonefield inventories there is also a single mention of the word 'nakkit' or knead kit, again a word unknown in Staffordshire dialect sources, but referenced from Yorkshire.[60]

The most frequent relevant reference, in 27 probate inventories, is the presence of one or more meal arks.[61] Most of the examples existing recently in the area, now destroyed but described by their owners, were crudely-made oak plank chests,

Left: Cooling oatcakes is an important part of their making but equipment for cooling is not identifiable from probate inventories because it was not specialised. Large farms had wooden ceiling racks which were also used for storing food and airing clothes. Small-scale domestic makers used a bowl or an upturned chair. Modern oatcake-makers have sophisticated metal racks, some with swivelling shelves.

Incidentally, when I was a child, I thought the pattern on the top of an oatcake was like my mother's legs – an intricate lace-work of scorch-marks made by sitting too near the fire in an otherwise freezing house.

Opposite: Hawking oatcakes round the streets in a basket was the usual method of selling them in the nineteenth century.

without internal separation, and without the typical sloping ark-shaped top. The clear space inside had the purpose, still remembered a few years ago, of storing oatmeal and bacon together. After salting and drying for about three weeks, the sides of bacon were layered in the ark with fine oatmeal. The ark was usually kept upstairs in the bedroom over the kitchen so it would be dry but not too hot. This form of storage enabled the bacon to be kept throughout the winter without going 'reasty' and gave it a fine white finish, while at the same time ensuring the oatmeal kept dry and prevented it from going sour.[62] This use is substantiated by some of the entries in the inventories. Meal and bacon were usually listed either individually or together with cheese, but they were occasionally inventoried along with the ark. Thus, from an inventory of the goods of William Mellor of Butterton, 1747, 'In the lower chamber – 2 beds £3 0s 0d; 1 chest 10s; 2 cofors 10s; 1 meal ark 15s; meal and bacon £3 0s 0d'. Arks were also occasionally inventoried along with meal but no bacon. Twelve inventories list more than one ark, the largest individual number being five; in this case, that of William Mellor of Butterton already quoted, one was in the upper chamber, one in the lower chamber, and three 'old arks' had been relegated to the stables.

That arks were specialised items, distinct from other similar pieces of furniture, is shown by entries such as the one from Thomas Mellor of Warslow, 1735: '3 meal arks, 2 cuppards, 4 coffers, 1 chest, 2 small boxes – totall £2–10s.'

Individually, ten arks were valued at 10s or under, and ten at between 10s and £1 0s 0d. The most expensive was £1 5s 0d, the cheapest 4s. The inventories where arks are mentioned were all connected with farmers, usually of some standing, as we can see from the total value of their possessions:

Numbers of inventories	Value of total goods
9	Over £100
13	Between £20-£100
5	Below £20

Pointing to the incompleteness of the probate inventory evidence is the 1725 record of Richard Bonsall of Westside; this farm inventory did not list a meal ark, though there was a seemingly original seventeenth-century oak ark built into the loft of Westside when William Bonsall sold the farm in the winter of 1972 (see p.53).

As with arks, the wills mentioning bakestones were also connected with farmers, with the single exception of the widow Sarah Bagshaw of Shiningford; in this case there is no inventory but the will itself specified her belongings – 'a chaff bed and bedding, a little table, one iron bakestone and a burnt iron' – left to her nephew.[63]

In summary, the inventory evidence, though not mentioning oatcakes by name, clearly relates to an oatcake tradition. This was not, of course, restricted to the Staffordshire moorlands. Similar evidence can be found from all over the Pennine world – for example probate inventories from the moorland fringes near Stockport give us records of baxstons, backe spittells and deshens (William Norton of Stockport, 1615/16).[64]

The oak meal ark from Westside Farm, Hulme End

Although home-made, the substantial oak planks were originally hand-sawn to very accurate tolerances, possibly by itinerant professional sawyers. All the planks are loose-fitted with simple v-joints which could accommodate movement of the timber. Such a construction means the heavy piece of furniture could be dismantled easily and moved. It was found in the second-floor loft of the Westside farmhouse, Hulme End, the home of the Bonsall family for many generations.

According to Bonsall family tradition, the Westside chest was used for storing salt bacon: the sides of bacon were steeped in brine and saltpetre on the salting stone in the back kitchen, for about two weeks; they were then hung up to dry for a further two weeks and then put into the chest to cure. A layer of oatmeal was placed in first, then one side of the bacon, then more oatmeal, then the second side and a final layer of oatmeal pressed firmly down, to expel air. Both bacon and oatmeal were thus kept airtight.

It is this last stage of filling an oatmeal chest which was remembered by F. Marian McNeill from her childhood in Scotland: 'In my childhood, when the sacks of meal came back from the mill to the Manse (for we grew our own oats) we smaller children used to have our feet washed and thoroughly dried, and were lifted onto the top of the meal to tramp it down, which we did with great gusto.'

(Oral information given by William Bonsall, 1972; F. Marian McNeill, *The Scots Kitchen; its Traditions and Lore with Old-time Recipes*, Blackie, London and Glasgow, first published 1929, 2nd edn 1963, p. 209)

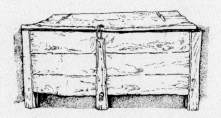

Meal ark from Westside Farm

SEVEN

'Shaped like gramophone records'
Memories from the moorlands

O NE OF THE STRIKING FEATURES of Staffordshire moorland life which emerges from the inventories is its stability over time. Many of the family names which figured in the eighteenth-century wills still occurred in the same farmsteads in the late twentieth century. One might, therefore, reasonably expect a high rate of survival over this intervening period of both the tradition of oatbread-making and the associated physical objects. One retrospective account from Wincle confirms this. Whilst working on a moorland farm in the 1940s, J. H. Ingram wrote down the reminiscences of his employer, Tom Mullins, who had been born in 1863:

> Little wheat bread was eaten. We lived mainly on oatmeal which was made into flat, sour oatcakes shaped like gramophone records. A cream-stean filled

Opposite: Bacon was an important component of Staffordshire diet and of the oatcake tradition. Here a Rugeley family celebrates the killing of their pig in time for Christmas, 1910. (Staffordshire Arts and Museum Service)

with oatmeal and water with a little sour dough to start it fermenting was left to stand for twenty-four hours. Every house had its 'bakston', a brick fireplace with a circular iron top, standing besides the kitchen range. When the iron top was hot it was greased with a little fat, and enough oatmeal mixture to make a thin cake was poured on it. They cooked in about three minutes, and usually enough were made at one baking to last a week or ten days. By that time they would be covered with a green, furry mould, which would be scraped off so that they could be toasted before the fire and eaten with butter or cheese. There was nothing better you could wish for.[65]

Tom Mullins also remembered the 'meal ark' and the connection between bacon and oatmeal:

Hams were not smoked, but after being hung up to dry for two or three weeks they were put in the 'meal ark', a great oak chest nine feet long and a yard wide, in which the oatmeal was kept. The hams were buried out of sight in the meal, and were thus kept airtight until required.

Although few written accounts like this have survived, I came across many such memories when I set out into the moorlands in the 1970s, asking about oatcakes. I soon found enough oral evidence to show that domestic oatcake-making similar to that described by Farey and Mullins was still fairly common amongst farms and cottages in the moorland area after the Second World War. The tradition was similar, but not identical. Oatcakes were now usually made only in winter and as a weekend luxury rather than a staple. Bought 'leaven' (i.e. yeast, dried or brewer's barm) was used instead of the old method of 'souring' by leaving some of the previous dough mixture in the bowl. The newer recipes were made with water or a mixture of milk and water instead of the buttermilk often used previously. They included, too, a little wheat flour as well as oatmeal. In 1996 a 92-year-old informant from Hollinsclough fixed this last change as taking place around the beginning of the twentieth century; as her mother told her that in the 1880s and '90s oatcakes were still made without wheat flour.[66] It is interesting that this is an example of the more general supplementation of other cereals by wheat which was a widespread trend throughout Europe from the Middle Ages onwards.

Opposite: Front and back views of Westside Farm, Hulme End. Photograph taken 1890–1900. From this house there is inventory evidence of a fixed bakestone and a surviving meal ark. (Thanks to Michael P. Grace and Tim Eades)

There are a number of interesting details in these photographs. For example, the girl sitting down (top) is sitting on the well. In the lower photo the back door supports a gritstone tank for collecting rainwater from the roof and propped up against the gable wall is a tin bath.

Lying in the angle of the dry-stone wall is a large sow. The building to the right is the dairy – evidence of the close association between oatcake, cheese and bacon.

Iron hanging or standing bakestones of up to 24 inches in diameter survived in fair profusion and were still occasionally used postwar. Fixed bakestones were still being built new as late as 1894.[67] Today, they have fallen prey to kitchen modernisation schemes and most have been taken out within the last seventy odd years, though one or two have survived. They are remembered as being used only for oatcakes and pikelets.

Iron slices and oak sprittles have survived in fair number, and in the 1970s many farmhouse kitchens had a set hanging up somewhere, if only for decoration. Most sprittles are about 12 inches square, with a flat handle, but some are larger, perhaps 18 or 24 inches square, to accommodate the traditional size of the old rural oatcake, which informants from Hollinsclough remember as being up to ¼ inch thick, soft and pliable, about 16 inches in diameter, similar perhaps to the medieval Welsh oatcake which were 'as broad as from the elbow to the wrist'.[68]

When is a pikelet not a pikelet?

The traditional commercial oatcake-maker made only oatcakes and perhaps also pikelets. There are even more arguments about pikelets than about oatcakes. Today Potteries pikelets look rather like small, thick oatcakes, but they are made with wheat flour, no oatmeal, a little sugar and sometimes dried fruit. But the nearest to the pikelets of my childhood memories are Welsh Pikelets (made only of plain wheat flour, eggs, butter and milk, no yeast or sugar). Interestingly, the name pikelet seems to derive from a Welsh word – 'pyglyd'.

(For these various recipes for different pikelets see www.cakebaker.co.uk)

Westside Farmhouse as it is today.

As far as mixing the leaven is concerned, the 'dashon' seems to have disappeared in actuality and in name, if not in memory. This is not surprising if they were coopered tubs which would fall apart quickly once they stopped being used. But the process of souring oatcakes was still within living memory in the 1970s. In the more isolated farmsteads around Hollinsclough a numbers of farmers' wives remembered their mothers leaving about two inches of old

A memory of Marston Montgomery

Pile 6 oatcakes on top of each other, each spread with meat dripping. Then cut like a cake.

Oatcakes in hell

Oatcakes can take you into some terrible places. William Farey's account of oatcake-making at Pilsbury, published in 1813, finished with a mention of 'soured oatcakes' being eaten by apprentices at a cotton mill at Litton, in Millers Dale near Buxton. Litton Mill, situated in a spectacularly beautiful wooded dale, became notorious in the 1840s for the appalling treatment of apprentices taken from workhouses in London and elsewhere. Several poignant accounts

have survived in newspapers and journals. John Birley, for example, was interviewed about his experience as an orphan boy working in Litton Mill and later at a mill higher up the Dale at Cressbrook. John described how, aged between six and seven, he was taken from the Bethnal Green Workhouse to serve as a parish apprentice at Litton. One of a group of twenty, John arrived at Litton late one evening, to be given a supper of oatcake: 'We were very hungry but

could not eat it. It was Derbyshire oatcake, which we had never seen before. It tasted as sour as vinegar.'

Their daily routine started at five in the morning and lasted until nine or ten at night. They had a breakfast at eight or nine, which consisted of: 'water-porridge, with oatcake in it and onions to flavour it. Dinner [midday] consisted of Derbyshire oatcakes cut into four pieces, and ranged into two stacks. One was buttered and the other treacled. By the side of the oatcake were cans of milk. We drank the milk with the oatcake in our hand, we went back to work without sitting down ... Supper was the same as breakfast – onion porridge and dry oatcake.'

The account went on to describe the beatings inflicted on him, one so severe that even the beater, the master's son Frank Needham, was frightened that he had killed him. John stayed at Litton for about three years until the owner, Ellis Needham, went bankrupt. He was then moved to Cressbrook Mill which had a better reputation but where he was also beaten with hazel sticks. He worked there until he was around seventeen years old. Litton Mill burnt down in the late nineteenth century, but was rebuilt. The photograph shows the mill in 2009, ironically now converted to luxury apartments.

(*The Ashton Chronicle*, 19 May 1849 quoted in www.peaklandheritage.org.uk)

leaven in the bottom of the mixing steen or panchion.[69] This was done only in winter when oatcakes were made regularly once or twice a week, the leftover leaven being nicely mouldy with wild yeast in two or three days. It would remain in this state only about a week in winter or a couple of days in summer, so that if the housewife did not make oatcake regularly she had to buy in yeast. This process of 'souring' seems to have come to an end about the time of the First World War, when bought yeast finally took over, though some home oatcake-makers managed without yeast until the 1950s, using bicarbonate of soda and cream of tartar.[70]

An important feature of the rural tradition as remembered in the farmhouses was the way the oatcakes were eaten. Although by the 1970s they were a Sunday treat, they were remembered from the moorlands in the early twentieth century as being just the opposite – a staple eaten during the week, while the weekend treat was wheat bread. Oatcakes were always provided at funerals, a testament to their long history and their place in the community. Interestingly, this same change, from a staple to weekend and special-occasion treat, was recorded in relation to oatbread by Minwel Tibbott working in Wales, only there the tradition eventually came to a complete end:

> Until the beginning of the nineteenth century oatbread was an essential 'survival food', especially to the small farmer and cottager, but with new developments in agriculture, and gradual changes in the diet of the rural population, its role was changed, and it was thus regarded as a 'festival food' [eaten on Sundays] for a short period before it became totally extinct.[71]

Generally, oatcakes were remembered from the moorlands as being served cold or heated in the oven. They were thick enough to be cut in half and toasted

'We grew the oats, took them to Brund Mill to be ground for the cows, but always had one bag ground finer into real fine oatmeal for oatcakes, though it still had a bit of the husk in it.'

(Frank Yates, Alstonefield, extract from *Voices from the Edge*, Staffordshire County Council, 2008)

Adding the flour

'Mother baked every day when we were children because she baked oatcakes over the fire. She use to get so much medium oatmeal and she put it in, say a gallon of water – or six quarts – and it was warm water – new-milk warm. And a bit of salt – and she worked it with her hands. And then she used to put about a cupful of flour in. If you didn't put a bit of flour in you couldn't turn them – they were too rough. And Mother hadn't a bakstone, she had to do hers over the fire and she had a thing made – smithy made … There were two or three bars and it fitted onto the back of the grate – there was a little ridge and just fitted on. Then she'd have a wooden back-spriddle. She'd make a pile high.'

(Mrs Gertie Mellor, formerly of Hollinsclough; extract from S. Gaukroger, *The Farmer's Wife*, History Live Publication, June 1993)

on a fire-bar toaster or fork, or broken into pieces to soak up the last juices of lobby – the equivalent of the old medieval potage. They were eaten with almost anything that was going – sweet or savoury, meat or vegetable – but most usually with lard or cheese, and favourite of all with children, syrup or jam. For one man, a farmer in Glutton Dale near Longnor, the preferred way of eating them was warmed and topped with a pile of buttery mashed potato. The ultimate in luxury was to dip them into the tin of meat juices standing under the bottle-jack on which the meat joint was roasting. They could be kept for several days in a pile in the pantry, the pile turned over every day and the top one used.

Derbyshire oatcake

In 1970, the rural oatcake of the Staffordshire moorlands of the early twentieth century was remembered as being thick and large, so thick it could be cut and toasted in a firebar toaster or broken into pieces like wheat bread.

The recipe below is probably the nearest to the old moorland oatcake. It was published in 1931 as Derbyshire Oatcake and was then claimed to be the same as that in use in 1811. From Florence White, ed., *Good Things in England*, originally published 1931, The Cookery Book Club, 1968, pp. 78–9.

2lb fine oatmeal

1 quart (32 oz) water

½oz barm or compressed yeast

Put barm or yeast into the water which must be warm

Put all into the meal

Mix by hand till smooth

Leave mixture to stand for 2 hours

Pour a cupful on to a hot stone (a baking tin or frying pan, if no stone is available)

Turn the cake so that it is done on both sides

When cold cut into four and butter

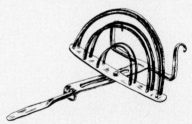

Firebar toaster used for toasting oatcake, from Sheen, now in Staffordshire Arts and Museum Service

Oatcakes, socks and sunburn

'Mother made about forty-five oatcakes a week in the winter. They'd start on Thursday morning and she'd get a big 'gell' (a sort of deep jar, different from a pancheon – they were earthenware outside and glazed inside) They mixed meal, warm water, a bit of flour, yeast, so much milk in the gell and she stirred it with the length of her arm because it was so deep. Then she'd heat the fire up, a good red fire and put the bakstone which … fitted over the fire. Then she'd put a cupful of this mixture on – after it had stood a while and started to go frothy – and then she'd sit down to knit a sock. She'd knit one round of the sock, then turn the oatcakes with the back-sprittle, then another round of the sock and the oatcakes were done. She put them on three upturned basins, rotating them, and the moisture which ran down the basin she used to put in a bottle and that was very good for sunburn – the oatmeal water. And that was how she did it – by knitting socks and making oatcakes she was doing two jobs at once.'

(Mrs Mavis Moore, formerly of Chelmorton, extract from S. Gaukroger, *The Farmer's Wife*, History Live Publication, June 1993)

EIGHT

Stokers' ovens and stick fires
Oatcake-eating in the Potteries

L ARGE-SCALE DOMESTIC OATCAKE-MAKING in the rural moorlands declined with the demise of living-in farm servants who had to be fed by the farmer's wife. Today it is the urban areas south-west of the moorlands which keep the oatcake truly alive. This transition from a rural to an urban context is intriguing. Was the oatcake-eating tradition of the Potteries an import from further north in the county or a remnant of a previous rural diet? The map of the 1801 crop returns shows clearly that oats were grown with other cereals in many parts of the county, perhaps for livestock feed; but what of human food? Crucially, there is evidence of an oatcake tradition within the geographical area of the Potteries before the process of industrialisation had fully developed. This comes from country-house records, not because the eating of oatcakes was more important at this level of society than others but because housekeepers working in country houses kept good account books in which they recorded

The grim face of the Potteries in the 1930s The back yards of Lower John Street, Longton. (Potteries Museum Photograph William Blake)

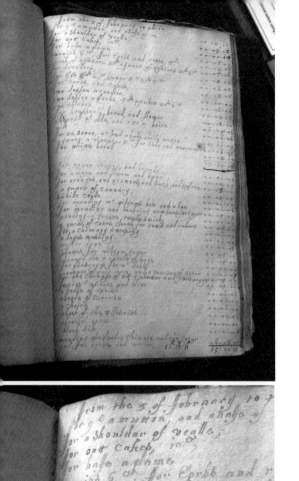

the relatively insignificant details of everyday life.

The household account book kept by Mrs Frances Sherrington, the housekeeper at Trentham Hall in the 1670s and 1680s records many purchases of oatcakes. During the week 3rd to the 10th of March 1678/79 for example, Mrs Sherrington bought tenpenny worth of oat-cakes.[72] But the most numerous records come from the household accounts of John Fenton of Shelton Hall between 1683 and 1694. These include fifty-one entries relating to oatcakes.[73] Most of the entries date from the years 1690 to 1693, during which time they occur

The account book of Mrs Sherington, housekeeper at Trentham. Entry for the week beginning 3 February 1678.
(Staffordshire Record Office, D593/R/1/6/4)

once, twice or even three times week, mainly but not exclusively during the summer months – perhaps bought in for feeding summer labour on a farm. The earlier entries are all for the purchase of oatcakes along with other goods such as turnips, dutch thread, tobacco pipes and oil of vitriol. From May 1693, however, payments were made to a single woman called Ellen Asbury, for baking oatcakes; it is not clear where this baking took place, whether in her own house or in the hall kitchens. In August the same year there was a payment made for drying a kilnful of oats, which may or may not relate to the baking. The account usually refers to 'oatcakes' but there are two references to 'oat bread'.

These references to oatcakes in the accounts of well-to-do or aristocratic households are important. They show that even in the late seventeenth century there were oatcake-makers operating on some sort of commercial basis, even if only on a small scale, within the area which later became urbanised. In addition, the food historian Peter Brears has made the point that recipes for oatcakes can be found in the accounts of even the wealthiest of Yorkshire families and that oatcakes were not solely a cottage or farmhouse item.[74] In the context of a wealthy household were oatcakes bought for family breakfast or as a staple for servants?

Further evidence supports the idea that oatcakes in the Potteries date from before industrialisation was fully developed. The 1725 probate inventory search described earlier revealed four references from this same geographical area to farmers owning one or more oatbread utensils – bakestones, sprittles and slices. There is also one printed reference from 1796, in William Pitt's account of the agriculture of Staffordshire:

The quantity of wheat raised in the county (exclusive of seed for next year), is sufficient only for ... 2/3 of its present population ... The deficiency is made out by purchase from other counties and by oatbread, which is eaten in considerable quantities in the north of the county, and in the Potteries, though scarcely known in the south.

The very nature of the urbanisation of the Potteries lent itself to the retention of a hitherto rural tradition such as oatcake-eating. In the seventeenth and early part of the eighteenth century the area now covered by the Potteries was still a group of villages south of the moorland edge, with rural areas between and around them. The pottery industry developed in its early phases in very small-scale units, often part-time, which served to preserve its rural character, remnants of which could still be seen well into the twentieth century.

As the area became more and more industrialised, the population of the Potteries increased. But how much of this growth was due to an increasing birthrate amongst the existing population and how much to immigration by people from outside the area who might have brought new food habits? David Gatley has calculated that between one-third and one-half of the population increase of Hanley between 1811 and 1851 may have been due to immigration rather than natural increase.[75]

Yet most of the people moving into the area for work came from nearby surrounding areas; well over three-quarters of the population of Hanley were either born in the town or within ten kilometres. So, the population had local, often rural, origins, despite its increasing dependence on the pottery industry. Many incomers must have moved from the nearby poorer farming areas to the north – that is the moorlands – bringing their taste for oatcakes with them

Above: Shelton Old Hall, the home of John Fenton. (Trustees of the William Salt Library)

Below: even recently, the Potteries landscape was an amazing intermingling of the industrial and the rural. This pastoral scene of Shelton Farm was very close to Hanley town centre, with Swynnerton Pottery and St Mark's Church in the background. Also nearby in the 1950s, when this view was taken, was a slaughter house. At this later time the fields were used as lairage for animals awaiting slaughter. (Potteries Museum)

Two illustrious sons of Staffordshire

Dr Johnson, in his dictionary, defined oats as 'a grain, which in England is generally given to horses, but in Scotland supports the people' – perhaps not to be taken (as has often been the case) as a derogatory remark about the Scots, but merely a matter of fact. In any case it was not an original remark – the Greek physician Galen made a similar point about oats and horses and the doctor would certainly have been familiar with Galen's writings. In his account of his journey to the Western Islands of Scotland he described Scottish oatcakes as 'very thin cakes, coarse and hard, to which unaccustomed palates are not easily reconciled'. Perhaps it was the hardness which Dr Johnson disliked for he was familiar with Staffordshire oatcakes, as we know from James Boswell's record of an occasion when staying with him at an inn in Lichfield: 'I saw here for the first time, oat ale; and oat cakes, not hard as in Scotland, but soft like a Yorkshire cake, were served at breakfast. It was pleasant to me to find that "*Oats*", the "*food of horses*" were so much used as the *food of the people* in Dr Johnson's own town.'

(Johnson, Samuel, *A Dictionary of the English Language*, 1833 edition, vol. II, p. 215; Johnson, Samuel, *A Journey to the Western Islands of Scotland, 1775*, ed. J. D. Fleeman, Clarendon Press, Oxford, 1985, p. 44; *Boswell's Life of Johnson*, ed. George Birkbeck Hill, Oxford, 1934, vol. II, p. 463)

Josiah Wedgwood, out journeying on a hot summer's day, could not find a pub. 'All we could meet with was a little mouldy oatcake, cheese fill'd with caraway seeds and some small beer, all of which we begged from a workman.'

(Meiklejohn, *English Domestic Medicine in the Eighteenth Century*)

The Oatcake-maker and the witch

'In the early nineteenth century, a witch was said to live at Gettliffe's yard in Derby Street, Leek. Two old women lived in the yard on very friendly terms. The one made a legitimate living baking and selling oatcakes; the other practised as a fortune-teller and a black and white witch. The witch owned a black cat that was mistrusted by the people who lived in the yard; they thought it was inhabited by an evil spirit. The woman who baked oat-cakes noticed that, whenever the cat was present, her baking went wrong. One day when the cat was there, and the woman's temper had been tried too far, she threw a partially baked hot cake at the creature. The scalded animal went crying into the witch's house, and the woman followed, determined to tell her friend what she thought of her pet and its tricks. Once inside the cat was nowhere to be seen, but the old woman had a bad burn on her back and was crying out with the pain.'

(Jon Raven, *The Folk Lore of Staffordshire*, 1978, p. 37 (From a story in 'Old Times in Leeke'))

and reinforcing the already established tradition. In many respects the Potteries retained the character of a cluster of overgrown villages rather than a centralised town, a feature which may have helped the survival of oatcake-eating.

Perhaps the most important source of information about the diet of the working people of the Potteries in the early nineteenth century comes from factory commission reports. These give brief glimpses of pottery children's diets, in evidence taken more or less verbatim from over three hundred 8 to 14 year

A very silly story

'Sarah Ann Cornwall charged Ann Cork with an assault. The parties are neighbours in Longton, but, as it appeared, living on anything but neighbourly terms. The complainant had a plaster on the forehead in consequence of a wound which she said had been inflicted by the defendant, but she could give no other reason why she had been thus assaulted than that the defendant had called after her 'oat cake and cheese' and she retaliated by calling her 'herrings and treacle.' (Laughter) The defendant's plea was that she did all she could to annoy her, and every time on passing her house called out 'five months and a bit.' This it turned out on explanation had a very significant meaning. As to the injury on the complainant's fore head, a witness for the defence said she got it by falling against a wall when the defendant hit her on the back. Mr. Glover considered that there was 'six of one and half a dozen of the other,' and the result was that each was ordered to find a surety of £10 to keep the peace for six months.'

(*Staffordshire Advertiser*, 17 January, 1863)

olds, obviously uneducated and over-awed by the enquiry.[76] The most common breakfast dish was 'milk meat' (white bread crusts soaked in water and milk) and the next most common was bread and tea. Dinner at midday for most of the children was 'sometimes beef or bacon and taties', with a fair number having dry potatoes and salt most days, and others having milk meat or 'stir pudding' (more commonly called hasty pudding, boiling milk with flour poured into it).[77] Oatbread is never mentioned by them, but oats do figure in the form of what the children called 'water peeps', described by one of them as oatmeal and hot water. This was a common breakfast dish for some of the children.

One important point emerges from these testimonies. It is clear that there was a heavy dependence, in some cases almost total, on potatoes, with a supplementary dependence on white 'bakers'' bread, probably highly adulterated. This fact is illustrated by one witness to the commissioners:

> Supervisor of the painting room: 'I know of one family living near me of eight, the man gets 6s 0d a week; the woman came to me last Saturday and I asked her how she lived: she said that with the 6s 0d she bought a stone and a quarter of flour and a peck of potatoes; this lasted till Thursday night, then with the 1s 0d she earned by washing she bought a brown loaf for 6d and another peck of potatoes, which would do again till Saturday. I don't know how she paid her rent. In Hanley there is plenty such.'

Oatcake-makers do not appear in trade directories in the nineteenth century or even the early decades of the twentieth. In a Burslem directory for 1904, for example, there were 30 fish and chip shops but not a single oatcake-maker. We have to wait until 1924 when Mrs Mary Preston appears in 56 Pleasant Street as a pikelet-maker.

In 1932 there were 2 oatcake-makers in Burslem directories, both in Waterloo Road, and a pikelet-maker in Wharf Street ... In 1940 one of the oatcake-makers had become a 'pastry cook'.

This diet might have been extreme but it is clear that potatoes were the single most important food item. Other sources tell us that potatoes had become a major element of the diet of both the moorland areas and the Potteries. In 1796 William Pitt described the potato crops from Dilhorne, a parish between the Potteries and Leek:

> [They] essentially contribute to the comfortable support of many thousands of manufacturers in Mr Wedgwood's beehive of commercial industry, the Pottery.[78]

Poor quality white bread was also important in the diet of working people of the Potteries. Oatbread would, in fact, have been a substantial improvement. In the neighbouring county of Derbyshire, for example, the miners realised this only too well, as was noticed by Sir Humphrey Davy in 1813:

> The Derbyshire miners in winter prefer oatcakes to wheaten bread: finding that this kind of nourishment enables them to support their strength and perform their labour better.'[79]

As with the Parliamentary reports, hospital records give no specific mention of oatcakes, though in the matron's accounts for Stafford General Infirmary for 1800 there are records of the purchase of large quantities of oatmeal: each week saw the purchase of two half-strikes at seven shillings each. Since twenty stone of bread was also bought, it is likely the oatmeal was made up into a porridge-like oatmeal-based gruel rather than oatcakes.[80]

As far as workhouse diets are concerned, we know from national sources that oatmeal did in fact provide an important staple. Peter Higginbotham, who has studied many aspects of the workhouse, found that before the New Poor Law of 1832, the old workhouses established by local parishes generally reflected local traditions of food, so that oatcakes might well have been bought or made. From 1835 onwards, workhouses adopted a more uniform, regulated system of food allocation.[81]

Oatmeal, in fact, provided a problem for those concerned with workhouse food supply. As we have seen, its dietary advantages were well known even at that time. But surprisingly it was relatively expensive, the wholesale price of oatmeal being 17s 6d a hundred-weight in the mid-nineteenth century. A contractor tendering to supply oatmeal to workhouses in London found that his prices, which he thought fair, were always 4s above everyone else's:

This was a mystery to me. By accident I found oatmeal was adulterated with barley-flour which is bought at about 7s per cwt; this being mixed with the oatmeal, of course reduced the price. I then, being as wise as my competitors, tried and have served the above workhouse since.[82]

St Monday

'During Saturday night, Sunday and Monday, they fared sumptuously. On Tuesday little was left, but from Wednesday to the following Saturday night they had what they could get, and so were next to starvation ... I have known this same woman to invite two or three of her pals in to tea on the Monday, send for half a pint of rum to be put in the tea, and make pikelets for the lot. As the last-named came from the bakestone she would tell the women to butter them, remarking, "Put plenty of butter on, our Jack will get two pounds this week."'

(T. Hawley, *Sketches of Pottery Life and Character, 1840–1850*, p. 26)

Adulteration of commercial oatmeal was, in fact, widespread. By comparison the farmers of the Staffordshire moorlands, relying as they did on their own supplies, were well off. The story about workhouse tendering is also a timely reminder that oatmeal was not popular as fuel for work people because it was cheap – William Pitt found in Leek in 1796 it was little cheaper than wheat flour – but because it was filling, energising and hardy in growing.

I have found one reference to oatcake-makers in the Potteries which fills the gap in information from the early decades of the nineteenth century. The Burslem pottery manufacturer Enoch Wood saved a satirical poster dated 1821 which ridiculed those shopkeepers who were criticising the system known as 'truck' – paying workers in goods rather than cash. The poster laid down rules of 'The Radical Society of Shopkeepers and Others', and one of the rules stated:

That makers and sellers of oatcakes, penny pies, black pudding, tripe, cow-heels, toffy, and matches (especially fraudulently fiddling with weights and measures) should gain the special protection of the society.[83]

This clearly puts oatcake-makers in their place – at the bottom of the commercial ladder, along with other purveyors of street food.

This characterisation of oatcake-making as being amongst the lowest of working class occupations, one which baked at home without permanent specialised premises and sold goods in the street, meant that they were not included in trade directories. The earliest specific nineteenth-century record I have found of a professional oatcake-maker in the towns of North Staffordshire is in the census of 1851. This comes from Spout Street (now more elegantly named St Edwards Street), Leek, where a 79-year old spinster named Ann Kidd lived. She gave her occupation as 'oatcake baker'. A native of Eaton, she was living with her son, William Kidd, a 56-year-old widower who worked as a groom, and his 26-year-old son, George, a cordwainer. There are surely many other oatcake-makers in the census records, but at the present time it is impossible to search electronically under occupation rather than name, but perhaps family historians delving into the census will eventually find more.

We are left with at best a shadowy picture as far as hard evidence about oatcake-making in the Potteries of the first half of the nineteenth century is concerned. They should have been an important part of the diet of working people and they were certainly present. But they seem to have replaced by potatoes as the staple

Oats into straw

Mr E. J. Morris worked the Oak Farm, Alsager, in the 1920s and '30s. He kept a herd of Shorthorn cows, as well as pigs, and grew oats, wheat and rye. The straw business was an important part of the enterprise. Most days he sent a cartload of oatstraw to Adams' potbank in Tunstall, on the way using extra 'chain horses' which were hired from cottages on Kidsgrove bank to help him get up the steep hill. On the return journey he used to bring home horse manure from stables in the Potteries to enrich his fields.

The illustration (right) shows the picture on a Mornflake packet, a popular breakfast cereal of the time still in production today. It is a painting taken from an original photograph, showing a Mr Harry Mottram, who worked at Oak Farm for Mr Morris, and the farm's three horses, cutting and binding oats.

(From Mrs Beth Sutton, Bignall End. Photograph: Mornflake)

filler for meals eaten at home. As street food, however, and for take-out meals and snacks at work, oatcakes would have been far more convenient, and it is perhaps in this capacity that they survived into the industrial context.

For survive they did. By the later nineteenth century, at the beginning of the period covered by the memory of Potteries people living in the mid-twentieth century, oatcake-making seems to have been fairly well established within the industrial areas as well as the northern moorland villages. The traditional explanation is that oatcakes were a nourishing and tasty food, bought by women who worked in the pottery industry full-time and who had little time or energy for cooking, and indeed little domestic incentive, given the quality of their housing. The Potteries was always an area of low wages and widespread poverty; a poor man's food went with that character.

Oatcakes were, in fact, a useful form of fast food, long before chips appeared on the menu. The potters retained the old tradition of setting off for work with just a drink of tea inside them, breakfasting during the early morning, usually between 9.30 and 10.00. There was another break at midday. The only cooked meal was in the evening at home. According to Mervyn Jones writing in 1960, at the breakfast and midday breaks sandwiches, toast and pies were eaten:

POTTERY PACKERS.

The traditional way of transporting ceramics was to pack them with straw in basketwork crates. Casks were used mainly for exports. (Potteries Museum)

People visit their friends in other departments and eat in scattered groups – in workshops, stores, offices, ware-houses: along corridors, sitting on steps, or in the open.[84]

Although there is no mention of oatcakes in Jones' account, they would have made an ideal snack in these situations. Workers could warm the oatcakes on a stoker's shovel or on the steam pipes running through the works – a tradition which perhaps illustrates the contrast between the small, informal easily-accessible manufacturing units of the Potteries and the massive, highly-structured workplaces of the textile industries of Lancashire and Yorkshire. Tradition has it that the pottery kiln and its stoker's shovel is one of the reasons why oatcakes have remained so important in the Potteries. One thing is sure – oatcakes and potbanks go together. Later, when the larger pottery works had canteens, they often used to serve oatcakes for lunch.

We can perhaps see a clearer picture of the importance of oats in the Potteries by returning to the oats themselves and to some of their special properties, notably their superiority over other cereals for bedding and packing. Recent analysis of cropping acreages for cereals in Staffordshire show that from the 1870s onwards acreages planted under wheat and barley dropped severely, whereas those for oats stayed steady.[85] The reasons for this were associated not only with climate or soils but also with market demand. The pottery industry was heavily dependent on horse-drawn transport for marketing its goods, especially horse-drawn canal boats. Lots of horses meant a high demand for straw for bedding as well as rolled oats for feed. Moreover, oat straw is soft and low in dust, making it a good material for packing around the pottery sent off in crates, baskets and hogshead casks. The pottery industry thus had an insatiable demand for straw. Most mornings would see carts setting off to local markets to buy straw, especially from the area to the north-west of the Potteries. Cottagers on Kidsgrove Bank (a steep hill for those carts laden with straw coming back into the Potteries) made a living out of hiring extra horses to the carriers. Even the oat husks were used for packing pots. Cheap and light in weight, they were bagged up at the corn mills and sold to the pottery manufacturers. So what made the Potteries different from other industrial towns around the Pennines was a consistent demand for the by-products of oat-milling. The traditional oatcake-eating habit fitted snugly into this scenario.

The characterisation of oatcakes as a low-grade street food, made at home, needing little equipment and only a domestic level of skill, is presumably why the professional baking trade never made them.[86] Later, indeed, oatcakes became associated more with butchers than bakers. But the typical oatcake-maker of the late nineteenth century was an elderly widow who earned her living making a few dozen a day on an iron bakestone over a stick fire on the kitchen range, hanging them to cool on a rack or over a chair back, and selling them round the streets from a basket. A descendant of this tradition, a woman known locally as 'Polly Pikelet' was still working in Uttoxeter in the 1920s. Back in 1970, oral informants recalled oatcake-makers of this type living at the end of the nineteenth century in Leek, Longnor, Froghall, Leigh, Kingsley, Dresden, Longton, Hanley, the Meir and as far south as Rugeley.[87] The tradition seems to have spread even as far as Wilsmlow in Cheshire, where a relative of an informant is remembered from the 1890s as selling oatcakes around the streets using a very posh sprung pram, the oatcakes sandwiched between snowy white towels.

The reputation of oatcakes as 'common', as a poor man's food, reflected on the eater as well as the maker. They were an integral part of 'secondary poverty' – domestic mismanagement in a weekly cycle of dearth and plenty. Wages were paid on Saturday, so Saturday night and Sunday were associated with relative affluence and in the case of oatcakes with the delights of a Sunday breakfast. Thus the old rural tradition of eating oatcakes in the week but wheat bread at the weekend was turned on its head. Moreover, the pottery industry and the nearby mining areas were notorious for their observance of 'St Monday' – Monday being extension of and recuperation for the excesses of the previous days and nights – so oatcake-makers, like chip shops, did not open on Mondays but gradually built up their trade till the following weekend. This established the patterns of oatcake-making and -eating which remained throughout the twentieth century.

Rain and oatcakes go together. Adam Deakin from London Road Oatcakes, Stoke, on his stall at the monthly farmers' market, Stone, on a very wet Saturday in September, 2008. His stall was stocked with oatcakes (left in the photo below) and plain and fruit pikelets (right).

NINE

'A nice oatcake and a bit of local gossip'
Memories of the oatcake trade

THE PART-TIME FEMALE OATCAKE-MAKERS continued well into the twentieth century, when they either gradually declined into even smaller-scale makers, baking only a couple of dozen on a Sunday morning for a few pence, or their businesses developed into full-time enterprises. At the point at which these became commercially viable, it seems that often men took them over. By the early decades of the twentieth century many oatcake businesses were run by men or married couples. By the 1920s the two women making oatcakes full-time on their own in Fenton were unusual enough to be remembered, as were the two sisters-in-law who ran the oatcake shop in Longnor as late as the 1940s.[88]

A few makers still baked in their own kitchens but the development of technology was against them. As stoves (gas or later electric) gradually started to replace ranges it became awkward to use the old hanging or standing bakestones, which in any case were difficult to come by. Some people found ingenious solutions, such as using the solid shelf from an oven as a makeshift bakestone. All in all, it became easier to buy oatcakes than make them at home. For those prepared to make them for sale, the trade was developing and it became worthwhile to adapt part of their house into specialised premises – perhaps a

A minor problem of wartime

'Dear Mother,

Friday 24–11–1916

Thank you very much for your letter and parcel which I received alright the other day. Everything in it kept very well & as a rule we get everything alright. The oatcakes are the only things which are sometimes no good to eat because if they get hung up as they sometimes do through trouble in the Channel & we may be in the front line when we get letters and papers, they go mouldy but the pies are always in good condition. The fowl and sausage were very good & we got them the day after we came out of the trenches.

Ted Riley'

(From Katherine Bailey, ed., 'The Letters of Edward and Albert Riley, 1916–1918, *Audley & District Family History Society*, forthcoming)

back garden shack or in one case a coal-house stove built next to a heap of fuel. One at least had a brick-built slate-topped bakestone, but the fuel was now invariably coal. Other makers took to renting the front rooms of other people's houses, often in the poorest part of town, thus developing a shop frontage and selling through the window or door. They often lasted only a few months before moving on to another terrace or another trade. Others survived longer because they had a good site adjacent to a group of potbanks. 'The Hole in the Wall' in Hanley must have been one such site. The terraced house which forms the shop now was built by 1893 and the 1901 census records that there were three adults, including a bootmaker and a plumber, and six children living there. The house changed hands several times, but was established as an oatcake shop by the 1920s under the ownership of Lydia and Absalom Evans. Lydia's sister Elsie Eardley took over in 1935 and ran the shop with her husband until 1948. They sold it to two men, Francis Davis and Thomas Byrne, who sold in 1950 to Martin McNicholas. In 1963 his relatives, Mr and Mrs John Clarkson, took over and ran it for 20 years until it was bought by the present owner, Glenn Fowler, a former chip shop owner. Thus the business passed from one owner to another in the same premises. Today it incorporates a sandwich bar next door while in the past local tradition has it that the living room was used to sell drapery.

Mrs Brenda Kitching, now living in the Isle of Man, remembers her local oatcake shop in Tunstall in the 1920s, a terraced house at the top end of Paradise Street – a good central site. It was owned by a woman – 'a canny lady' of the name of Susan Roberts, known locally as 'Sooie'. Her oatcakes had a tremendous reputation in the town: 'Thay cost av oatcakes from all ower th' Pots, but thays nowt lark Sooies!'

As was usual, the shop was open only on Fridays, Saturdays and Sundays, which meant hard work but concentrated into the weekend. Sooie made enough money to retire early, in her fifties. Rumour spread about where she had gone to – 'sum wier on th' Welsh coost – Rhyl ar think' – which must have seemed like the Costa del Sol back in the 1920s.

Lockett's Oatcakes of Lightwood Road, Normacott, photographed in 1973. Note how the right-hand window has been altered. The shop was operated by two generations of the same family until 1961 when it was sold. The Lockett name in oatcakes was later taken up by a new shop. (www.thepotteries.org)

At the 'Hole in the Wall' the size of the window opening through which oatcakes are sold is unchanged since the house was built, but the original sash window has been replaced by a modern purpose-made inward-opening hinged casement. Even so, the sash windows provided in the nineteenth-century terraces must have been more suited to selling than the eighteenth-century-style outward-opening casements.

An outlet for the unemployed, oatcake-making was often taken up by default rather than by choice. One man went into the trade in the 1920s after quitting a skilled pottery job in disgust at his working conditions and wage fixing.[89] This man built up a thriving business still in production in the 1970s, by using his wife and children as distributors, hawking the oatcakes around the streets of Fenton in an orange-box on wheels. Others used a bike with a basket on the front. In a strange sort of mirror-image of the place of oats in the medieval village economy, oatcake-making was a useful fall-back trade – if you were near starvation and couldn't do anything else to earn a crust, you could make and sell oatcakes.

Market stalls were also used as outlets for oatcake-sellers. An informant who was aged 86 in 2008 remembered her childhood in the Meir, Longton. In 1927 she lived with her parents next door to her grandfather, Richard

Henry Hallam, in Uttoxeter Road. Her grandfather had a butcher's shop in Longton. On Fridays he used to make oatcakes and pikelets in a bakehouse behind his house. She would run home from school and hang around the bakehouse, watching him ladling the mixture and savouring the delicious smell. She would help him to wrap the oatcakes in white linen cloths and put them into large baskets which were loaded onto a trap ready for morning. Then she would go with him on the pony and trap to sell them in Longton market, along with his home-cured bacon.

A 'front room' oatcake shop.

Agnes Pearson with assistant and Barry Chawner at her oatcake shop in Unwin Street, Bradeley, April, 1986. Agnes owned the shop and Barry Chawner was an agent for Pearl Assurance who collected her insurance every Saturday morning. He always had tea in her lounge and took home some oatcakes. The bakery was in her front room, from where Agnes sold oatcakes over a counter, not through her window. Her living room was the backroom of the terraced house.

Unwin Street has long since been replaced by a new housing development, though the Talbot pub survives. (Photographs and information provided by Barrie N. Roberts)

Many of the people I interviewed in 1970 recalled the extreme poverty of the 1930s. Here are three extracts from one woman's memories of Hanley, when householders tried to earn a little extra money by selling oatcakes through their front-room windows or from a basket:

I remember several houses in the Botteslow Street and Waterloo Road area who had oatcakes for sale, spread out on tea towels on the front window sill – the sash window open about 12 inches. On Sunday mornings a young girl came to our house with hot oatcakes wrapped in a tea towel carried in a large wicker basket. We had a regular order.[90]

The Second World War brought several changes:

When the war came terraced houses seemed to stop making and selling them. Our supplies then came from Browns Butchers in Hanley Market and we ate them hot for tea spread with golden syrup, because bacon, cheese and eggs were rationed and very meagre in supply. Golden syrup was 'on points' but a tin lasted a while if you were careful. Bread was rationed later in the war, but oatcakes were exempt.

Rationing brought changes to the potbank dinner:

I liked to be around the kilns at dinnertime to see the men put their shovels in the fire to sterilise and heat them, then place an egg on the hot shovel to fry it, or more often an oatcake with cheese, and in summer and early autumn, tomato and sometimes bacon too. The poorer folk had the oatcake just hot and spread with margarine … wartime rationing put an end to the cheese, bacon and eggs.

It wasn't just chance that oats were not rationed during the war. In 1940, Professor J. C. Drummond, the government's famous Chief Advisor to the Ministry of Food on Food Contamination, submitted a memorandum which stressed the importance of increasing the general consumption of oats, along with high-nutritive bread, potatoes, cheese, milk and green vegetables. This memo

The advent of electric stoves made using a 'griddle' impossible. Here is one woman's solution.

A Christmas Tradition

'... hot, with freshly toasted cheese and newly cooked sausage, rolled, of course, to conserve the heat. This was the usual way of serving them on Christmas Eve in Leek when we were young and it was the traditional supper for the day and the occasion.'

(G. A. Lovenbury, 'Oatcakes', *Leek Post and Times*, 22 January, 1976)

provided the basis for what was in fact a highly successful food policy throughout wartime Britain.[91] The war, and the system of 'points' rationing introduced in 1941, forced people back to older foods – more cakes and puddings, more dishes made from leftover foods, and more oatmeal. Even that nineteenth-century stand-by, the gruel called 'hasty pudding', sometimes reappeared in wartime recipe books.[92]

Legislation as well as war brought changes. After the Food and Drugs Act of 1938 more capital investment was needed to meet new hygiene requirements and the oatcake trade stabilised. Gas-fired hotplates, still called 'stones' or 'bakstons', became standard after 1938. Wholesale distribution was introduced in 1946. In the 1970s there were 24 makers listed in the telephone book, selling both wholesale and retail in the Potteries, three of whom inherited their trade from relatives in the 1890s. Most were one or two-man businesses making only oatcakes and perhaps pikelets.

Besides changes in the trade, the twentieth century saw changes in the product itself – a development into what we now know as Staffordshire oatcake. It decreased in thickness and diameter from the original rural 16 inch cake to

Ye Olde Oatcake Shop Cheadle changed hands in 2008 but continues as a traditional oatcake-makers. Prior to this George and Betty Garner ran it for 16 years; they have moved to new premises in Weston Coyney.

The Garners have deliberately kept both shop and methods simple and it seems to work. A sandwich bar opening next door did not affect their trade – as George says 'If you want an oatcake, you want an oatcake not a sandwich.' Right: Mrs Betty Garner ladles the batter, giving each a quick circular movement with the back of the ladle. After turning them she removes them by lifting with a spatula and flipping them onto her hand.

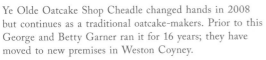

around 10 inches, as it was remembered from the 1920s, and around 8 inches by the end of the century. The addition of wheat flour and other raising agents also made it lighter and less likely to fall apart. Our modern Staffordshire oatcake is a refined version of what it once was but the change was progressive, not sudden, possibly driven by a number of factors – the need for a picnic-type lunch for industrial workers who preferred a thin oatcake, which could be easily rolled up, to the thicker version eaten by farm workers who sat down to dinner in the farmhouse kitchen; perhaps a change in taste and the desire for a more delicate flavour and texture by modern palates; or perhaps the pressures of commercialisation and the need to cut down on raw materials.

As early as the 1900s makers were working only Thursday, Friday, Saturday and part of Sunday, indicating that oatcakes had become a weekend tasty treat. This meant that even the hardest working of the full-time urban oatcake-makers never worked on a Monday. In the 1920s and 1930s and even into the 1990s oatcake-makers worked round the clock on Thursday and Friday nights, or began baking at 3 a.m., or worked on well past 2 a.m.[93]

The emphasis on weekend production meant that many makers found other jobs to boost income. Mr Hallam, who sold oatcakes on Longton market, was primarily a butcher in the town. Plants of Silverdale were also the excursion agent for the PMT (the main Potteries bus company).[94] The making, as we have seen of oatcakes seems to have been combined with butchery rather than bakery. I have come across only one reference to a professional baker making oatcakes and that was Mr Wright, the founder of Wright's Pies back in 1926.[95] Occasionally larger chains took up oatcake-making. In the 1950s Redmans, the grocers, used to make fresh oatcakes to order while you waited, in their shop in Hanley.

The habit of eating oatcakes for Sunday breakfast also coincided happily with

Castle Oatcakes in Newcastle is perhaps the most 'modern' of oatcake shops. Recently refurbished in stainless steel and glass, it occupies an outhouse behind a terraced house.

church-going. Smallthorne has had several oatcake-makers at different times. A later one was run by the Birch family, whose shop provided many memorable Sunday mornings for Mrs Lynne Bebbington. As the congregation from the Roman Catholic church in Brierley Street poured out of early morning mass, they made unerringly for the Birch oatcake shop.[96] A similar memory comes from Joan Dils who recalls the walk from the Sacred Heart R.C. Church to Waterloo Street and the Hole in the Wall.[97] Anticipation, as well as hunger, was sharpened by the requirement of the Catholic Church that communicants fast from midnight on Saturday until after mass on Sunday.

Top left: Oat Cuisine in Miles Green, near Bignall End. Unfortunately the shop front shown was damaged by a taxi and has had to be replaced. The corner site of a terraced street was a favourite traditional site for oatcake-makers.

Top centre: High Lane Oatcakes, Burslem

Top right: Lockett's shop in Dresden, now sold to Clarky's Premier Oatcakes, tucked in between other food takeaway shops.

Centre left: Weston Coyney Oatcakes, a brand new oatcake shop opening in the teeth of recession, sited in a small neighbourhood shopping centre.

Centre: Oatcake Annies, Fenton

Centre right: Oatcakes and Pikelets! in Chell Street, Hanley. Pikelets have been made alongside oatcakes since at least the nineteenth century, and usually come in a choice of plain or fruit. But here the choice has widened. The price board shows the shop also sells hot drinks and even fresh eggs.

Bottom left: Pittshill Oatcakes is a traditional oatcake-maker's shop sited in an area of older terraced property.

Bottom centre: Oatcake Kitchen, the shop run by The Original Oaties Company, Dresden.

Bottom right: London Road Oatcakes, Stoke, has a long tradition as an oatcake-makers, though it has changed hands several times and even moved from one side of the street to the other. Now owned by the Deakins who still make oatcakes by hand.

High Lane Oatcakes, Burslem, showing the huge bakestone with its machine at the far end. The oatcakes are still turned and removed by hand. The heat and the speed are phenomenal.

TEN

Oatcakes, football and the internet
The 21st century and beyond

DESPITE THE PROBLEMS OF THE HOLE IN THE WALL, surrounded as it is by blocks of new flats and modern housing, the stresses of the 'credit crunch' and the gloomy predictions of one website which proclaims the Staffordshire oatcake is in danger of dying out, I feel optimistic. The habit is spreading rather than declining and the existence of 40-odd oatcake shops augers well. The makers themselves seem cheerful – 'There'll always be a call for a good oatcake, it's a good steady trade', said one. With such diverse dietary choices facing us today, surely he is right. With the rising price of wheat bread, oatcakes are still a cheap meal. The whole history of oatcakes, after all, is of survival in times of the severest financial stress. And despite urban renewal and the decline of the pottery industry, the Potteries is still a place like no other.

The change from domestic to commercial production happened over a long period and, even today, commercial oatcake businesses are usually family concerns. Expertise and experience can go back many years and are highly valued. Even new people coming into the trade will make use of the skills of older makers. When he bought his business, Steve Povey wrote the recipe 'on the back of a fag packet', but he still employs a man who has thirty-five years' experience of making oatcakes. Similarly Kevin Deakin, who went into the trade to escape the stresses of a declining local pottery industry which required him to make repeated journeys to China, still uses Ray Ellis to make his mix. Ray was the previous owner of the London Road shop in Stoke; he and his mother between them ran it for over 40 years but his family involvement in oatcake-making goes back much further. His father started making oatcakes at home on a plate over the kitchen stove, but then moved on to a shop in Silverdale for many years; even his grandmother opened a shop in Penkhull, in premises which are now part of the Greyhound Inn. The same recipe has been in continuous use within the family and the present shop for over 100 years. In these ways traditions are handed on.

Oatcakes are nothing if not adaptable, however, and modern commercial oatcake-makers vary by technology, site and clientele. There are still a number of old 'traditional' makers, using relatively small gas-fired bakestones, pouring the oatcake batter by hand from a ladle – very precise, quick but with a gentle almost loving circular flip with the back of the ladle to settle it. These makers often make tradition a feature in their name – Ye Olde Oatcake Shop and Traditional Oatcake Shop.

There is one fully mechanised wholesale oatcake-maker on an industrial site in Loomer Road, Chesterton, but some of the retail makers have also adopted a degree of automation – for example a hopper machine which dispenses the batter in controlled amounts and which moves up and down a much longer bakestone. These have been available since 1982. Such machines make perhaps six dozen at a time; Povey's output is getting on for 10,000 per day and High Lane Oatcakes probably produce considerably more. The traditional makers operate on a smaller scale – perhaps 15,000 oatcakes a week – and they of course

Above: Povey's Oatcakes, Biddulph. Garry has been making oatcakes in North Staffordshire for 35 years.

Right: Alex, the owner's son, removing oatcakes onto a trolley. He is posing here, for his normal hand movement is lightening fast.

Steve Povey started in the 1990s: 'The proprietor went bankrupt and I took a gamble, rescued his machinery from his garage, copied the recipe from the back of an old fag packet, and the rest is history'.

Oatcake Annies, Fenton, early Sunday morning, 2008.

The oatcakes are hand-made. To the right of the entrance is a small sitting area. Some oatcake-makers have diversified, making sandwiches and hot drinks too.

decry the machines: 'The oatmeal has to be too fine or too diluted with flour to go through the machine, the batter has to have too much water in it, they give an uneven shape; the bakestones have to be too hot', and so on. Bakestones are still gas-fired but rising gas bills – thousands of pounds a month – are raising the possibility of conversion to infrared bakestones.

There is no doubt that oatcakes themselves are still changing. Many, though not all, machine-made cakes have become smaller, thinner and darker in colour than the handmade product, which to my mind is a worry. It is a continuation of the long-term trend towards smaller, thinner cakes made with increasing amounts of flour, so one has to ask the question: when is an oatcake still an oatcake? Yet there is no doubt a demand for the small, thin oatcake which many people prefer today. But it is not the traditional oatcake of the past.

The machines may help with the through-put but they have not replaced manual dexterity entirely. The speed and assurance with which the makers turn and remove the oatcakes using a metal version of the old sprittle is amazing. The dexterity of the old pottery workers is not entirely dead!

Dave Follows was the cartoonist beloved of the Potteries for his series 'May and Mar Lady'. In one cartoon he summarised the Pottery diet::

'Whuts up with thee, woman! Thay kneowst ah oweeys ave brine seowce not ketchup with me lobby, eowtceeks, payklets, wrayts pie, fish un chips, mushy pays un batter bits.'

Similarly the sites of oatcake-makers' shops vary. There are still some situated in older, run-down terraced properties, scheduled either for modernisation or demolition and facing, perhaps, the same stresses as the Hole in the Wall. Others, including the more mechanised ones, are in terraced shop areas, but in modernised high-street sites. Yet others have made the move to newer shopping courts. Businesses are fairly mobile, families moving from one site to another, but often the premises themselves remain as oatcake shops.

One reason for the mobility of oatcake-makers' premises is the changing nature of the industrial context of their neighbourhood. All of them need a good client base – not just small-scale off-the-street customers, but regular ordering from supermarkets, factories and other institutions. One factory closing down can effectively kill an oatcake business, just as can a road realignment; the creation of the new D-road (the A500) affected the trade in Stoke. Many supermarkets are supplied by Staffordshire Oatcakes Ltd, the wholesale oatcake factory, but shops like Povey's and High Lane also trade with supermarkets. The traditional London Road Oatcakes was once in a wonderful site, surrounded by potbanks and their workers, but even today it has a solid base, selling to staff from the nearby Michelin Tyre factory, Portmeirion Pottery, the main hospital site in North Staffordshire and three local farmers' markets. The Cheadle shop sells locally to shift workers from the nearby JCB factory but they also supply butchers' shops in Ashbourne and elsewhere. Mellors Oatcakes in Clayton is established in a suburban residential district, which dictates a wide diversification into sandwiches and drinks and like Cheadle, it is seeing a growing regular trade from schoolchildren coming in for breakfast. In some areas, the increasing numbers of immigrant families, not only from the Far East but also Eastern Europe, has added an exotic clientele that is familiar with flatbread of various types. Hence one oatcake shop in Tunstall survives in an area which is seemingly otherwise taken over by Asian food shops.

The breakfast trade is usually for filled oatcakes and many shops offer a variety of fillings. Povey's in Biddulph has 40 on the menu, including 'The Works' – 2 oatcakes with cheese, sausage, bacon, mushroom, onion, egg and tomato. Some even provide a sitting area for breakfast, useful for building-site and shift workers, while others have sophisticated websites for information and ordering. Some have gone down the 'branding' road, supplying their premises and their staff with colourful 'team wear' to

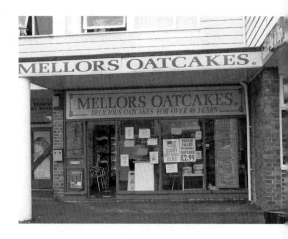

Mellors in Clayton is sited in a modern shopping terrace in a residential suburb and caters accordingly.

match the decor rather than plain white protective clothing. Marketing tricks allegedly include extractor fans which blow the smell down the street! The modern oatcake-maker who exploits the internet works longer hours – sometimes 6 days a week literally round the clock to keep up with demand.[98] Poveys operates three shifts to staff these long hours; two days a week they open for sales until midnight to supply shift-workers. Many open every day, Sunday morning still being very busy, though the smaller more traditional ones still close Mondays and Tuesdays. All of them open very early – from 6 or 7 a.m.

Most oatcake-makers are family businesses. The Original Oaties Co., Carlisle Street, Dresden, in their team strip. (www.staffordshireoatcakes.com)

Ingredients today are more sophisticated and precise than the old farmhouse materials and some contain raising agents unknown to the old farm wives.[99] Recipes are still secret despite the modern requirement to label packaging – but then it is the balance of ingredients which gives each oatcake its distinctive character rather than any 'secret' ingredient. Interestingly the 2009 consumer has reverted to an older way of eating oatcakes, with more varied fillings and at more flexible meals, eating oatcakes throughout the week, not just at weekends, but still mainly for breakfast or lunch. Oatcakes are after all highly suited to our takeaway food culture. They suit modern kitchen technology – not only do oatcakes microwave but they freeze well.

One feature which has also been changing is the social role of the oatcake shop in the Potteries. In some ways the local connection may be loosening.

A Yorkshire woman living in the Potteries contacted *The Sentinel* during the Hole in the Wall campaign in 2008 to describe how she enjoyed her weekly trip to Waterloo Street not just for the 'nice oatcakes' but also for 'a bit of local gossip'.[100] Another woman who used to work at the Hole described it as being 'at the centre of the community' in the 1960s.[101]

Such memories highlight what lies behind the passion shown by the campaign to save the oatcake shop in Hanley. The furore was not just about oatcakes or oatcake-makers but about a close-knit community facing up to the devastating changes wrought by urban renewal. As I stood outside the Hole in the Wall waiting my turn, I overheard a young woman who had just been told about the possible threat to the shop. 'Oh no', she said to the young man by her side, 'that's the last straw! Now they want to take away our oatcakes!'

There is no denying that oatcakes contribute widely to the urban character of the Potteries and perhaps all the more now that the old communities are breaking up or at least changing radically under urban renewal. Oatcakes figure in all sorts of unlikely places – the name of the Stoke City Fanzine, for example, and the 'Pottermouth's Battle Cry', a poem written by a contributor to Radio Stoke during the week in April 2008 when Stoke City Football team was fighting for promotion to the Premiership. On

Radio Stoke it was spoken in a flat Potteries accent to the tune of 'I vow to thee my country'. Endless requests on websites (even *The Guardian* website blog) also testify to the association made by nostalgic ex-pats between Potteries' culture and the oatcake. There is one ex-oatcake-maker from May Bank who emigrated to Australia thirty-five years ago and who has converted a trailer and goes around farmers' markets and fairs in the Perth area making fresh oatcakes.

So what have we learnt from our trawl through witnesses alive and dead?

Firstly, Staffordshire oatcakes have a much older pedigree than many would credit them with – older than the stoker's shovel or the Staffordshire Regiment and the Indian Raj and its chapatis. It is one of a whole host of regional food survivals which are a sort of time capsule, explaining our past to us if only we can take the trouble to tease out the detail.

Secondly, they reflect the geographical context of North Staffordshire with some precision – on the borderland between the midlands and the north. Before the industrialisation of the Potteries, oatcakes were not restricted to the moorlands proper but were made and eaten a few miles further south, there surviving the change from rural to urban environment.

Thirdly, the lesson of the oatcake story is that to survive you need to change; not necessarily progress or decline, but simply become slightly different. Over centuries, oatcakes have been changed in many ways – their size, texture, time of eating, place in the diet, equipment used, all practical adaptations to the requirements of the people making and eating them.

Finally, even a humble item of food can become a cultural icon of a community. Such markers of local character become even more important when under threat. There is after all a definite pattern to oatcake history: they provided a reliable food for the tough farmers of the moorlands just as they offered opportunities for emergency employment for the work-less of the Potteries. They were a blessing to the working mothers of the Victorian potbanks just as they are to the breakfast-less schoolchildren of today. Despite their appearance in country-house archives, oatcakes were always a friend to the poor rather than the rich and one of the reasons for their survival in the Potteries is the area's poverty and insularity over centuries. So is there a place for such a food in our spoilt-for-choice modern society? Will oatcakes survive the stresses of urban renewal, multi-culturalism, internet ordering, postal deliveries, global warming, obesity, the price of oil or bread, the credit crunch, recession? Oatcakes have been around a long time. Now they are super healthy. I wonder where they will take us next?

Recipes

A modern recipe for Staffordshire oatcake

> 8 oz (225g) fine oatmeal
> 4 oz (100g) each of wholemeal flour and plain flour
> 1 teaspoon each of salt and sugar
> ½ oz (15g) fresh yeast or 1 tablespoon dried yeast
> ¾ pint each (450ml) lukewarm water and milk
> Vegetable oil

With a wooden spoon work the yeast into ¼ pint (15ml) of the water. Add the sugar and stir well. Leave the mixture in a warm place for 10–15 minutes until frothy. Sieve the salt and both flours together in a warm bowl. Put the oatmeal into another bowl and then mix in the flour and salt. Mix well together. Add the remaining water/milk into the yeast mixture. Make a well in the dry ingredients and gradually beat the yeast liquid in. Cover with a warm clean damp cloth and leave to stand in a warm place for one hour.

Lightly oil a frying pan and put onto a high heat. Drain the pan, sprinkle with salt and wipe clean with a cloth. Ladle the mixture into the pan and spread by gently rocking the pan. Loosen with a spatula and cook until brown. Flip over with the spatula or toss, then press down lightly. When cooked, cool the oatcake on a wire rack over a bowl of cold water. Stack when cool. Will make 12 oatcakes.

(Thanks to www.poveyoatcakes.com)

An Italian version: Oatcake calzone

Spread the oatcake with a layer of thick tomato sauce previously heated. Cover with slices of Mozzarella cheese and sliced black olives. Grill until the cheese melts, then fold in half. Brush the top with olive oil and sprinkle with Parmesan cheese and black pepper. Serve with mixed green salad and chopped basil leaves.

(After www.oatcakes.org)

Not everyone is convinced

'They taste like soggy cardboard – what is all the fuss about?'

(www.bbc.co.uk/stoke)

Fish and broccoli bake

Make ¾pint of seasoned white sauce, reserve a small amount for the topping, pour the rest onto 8oz poached and flaked smoked haddock and 8oz lightly cooked broccoli. Grease a deep pie dish, put an oatcake on the bottom then a layer of the fish and broccoli mix, then another oatcake and so on, finishing with an oatcake. Pour the remaining white sauce over the top and sprinkle lightly with cheese. Bake at 180°C for 25–30 minutes.

A homemade oatcake recipe from the 1960s

3lbs plain flour
2lbs very fine oatmeal
½oz yeast
Salt
Luke warm water

Mix together and leave for 24 hours for the yeast to work. The volume will double – half a bucket will end up a full bucket.

(Thanks to Alsager Family History Society)

Heart attack sweet oatcake

Crumble a chocolate biscuit over an oatcake, add a generous dollop of lemon curd, roll it, microwave for a few seconds till the chocolate begins to melt, then drizzle a little honey on top.

Vanilla and jam oatcake – winner at the Stone Food and Drink Festival, 2008

Make a sweet sauce of plain flour, milk, vanilla essence and caster sugar. Leave to cool. Put jam or stewed fruit onto the oatcake, then spoon over the sauce. Fold it into an oblong and brush with egg white. Sprinkle with caster sugar and flaked almonds and bake for 5 minutes.

Ham-stuffed oatcake

Spread an oatcake with a mixture of chopped ham, mushrooms and parsley.

Fold in half and pour over the top some cheese sauce. Grill gently until the cheese sauce is bubbly.

Oatcake grill

This is the most common way of eating oatcakes nowadays. Simply spread grated or sliced cheese – traditionally Cheshire or Lancashire – over the oatcake and grill. You can add bacon or tomato or sliced sausage.

Lamb curry and oatcakes

Place an oatcake on the bottom of a pie dish, then add alternate layers of cooked lamb curry, oatcake and sliced bananas. Finish with curry sauce and bake for 30 minutes.

A Gazetteer of oatcake-makers

A. H. Short
62 Roundewell Street, Tunstall, ST6 5AN
01782 834926

Asplin's Oatcakes
2 Haywood Street, Leek, ST13 5JX
01538 387356

Barry's Pantry
66–66A, Crewe Road, Alsager, ST7 2HA
01270 872897

Box Lane Oatcakes
2 Box Lane, Meir, ST3 5PP
01782 319642

Bradwell Oatcakes
85–87, Hanbridge Avenue, Newcastle,
ST5 8HX
01782 662885

Brenda's Oatcakes
15 King's Street, Kidsgrove, ST7 1HW
01782 783841

Bucknall Oatcakes
254 Werrington Road, Bucknall, ST2 9AW
01782 204161

Burslem Oatcakes
9 Waterloo Road, Burslem, ST6 2EH
01782 819718

Cairns Oatcakes
46 Bagnall Road, Baddely Green, ST2 7AZ
01782 570144

Castle Oatcakes
78 London Road, Newcastle, ST5 1LZ
01782 662494

Clarky's Premier Oatcakes
287 Uttoxeter Road, Dresden ST3 5LQ
01782 321844

Congleton Oatcakes
28A Lawton Street, Congleton, Cheshire
01260 298040

Cornhill Oatcakes
41 Bemersley Road, Norton, ST 8JF
01782 542126

Fillers Oatcakes
155 Watlands View, Newcastle, ST5 8AW
01782 614835

Foley Oatcakes
421 King Street, Fenton, ST4 3EE
01782 599119

Oatcakes and Pikelets!
134 Chell Street, Hanley, ST1 6BD
01782 261899

G&E Garner, the 'O' Cake Shop
225 Beverley Drive, Bentilee, ST2 0NA
01782 269004/261899

Goldenhill Oatcakes
807 High Street, Goldenhill, ST6 5QH
01782 772441

Hamil Oatcakes
157 Hamil Road, Burslem, ST6 1AP
01782 818484

High Lane Oatcakes   *Pikelets?*
599 High Lane, Burslem, ST6 7EP
01782 810180

Hole in the Wall
62 Waterloo Street, Hanley, ST1 3PW
01782 261883

Hovis Oatcake Shop
61 Ford Green Road, Smallthorne, ST6 1NT
01782 811405

JB Oatcakes
4 East Terrace, Fegg Hayes, ST6 6QU
01782 823674

K & J Washington
5 Broadway Place, Meir, ST3 5PS
01782 319642

Knutton Bake & Take
8, High Street, Knutton, ST5 6DN
01782 866999

London Road Oatcakes
232 London Road, Stoke, ST4 5RH
01782 745059

May Bank Oatcakes
2 Oxford Road, May Bank, ST5 0JB
01782 621324

Mellor's Oatcakes
Cambridge Court, Clayton, ST5 3DA
07977805408

Mellor's Oatcakes
Heaton Terrace, Wolstanton

Mick's Grill
147 Whieldon Road, Fenton, ST4 4JG
01782 847409

Minton Oats
6 Rawlins Street, Northwood, ST1 6PE
07840625299/01782 206202

North Staffs Oatcake Bakers
Turner Crescent, Loomer Road Industrial
Estate, ST5 7JZ
01782 562804

Oatcakes Direct
35 Buccleuch Road, Normacot, ST3 4RJ
01782 314260

Oat Cuisine
96 Heathcote Road, Bignall End, ST7 8LL
01782 720641

Oatcake Annies
65 Victoria Road, Fenton, ST4 2HG
01782 411914

Oatcake Heaven
10 Hickman Street, Newcastle, ST5 2AR
01782 799888

Pittshill Oatcakes
104 St. Michael's Road, Chell, ST6 6LG
01782 835262

PN & JS
1a Fraser Street, Cobridge, ST6 3HR
01782 219430

Povey's Oatcakes
33 High Street, Biddulph, ST8 6AW
01782 511799

Sneyd Oatcakes
76 Milton Road, Hanley, ST1 6HD
01782 213105

The Original Oaties
8–10 Carlisle Street, Dresden, ST3 4HL
01782 313453

TJ Oatcakes
605 Leek Road, Hanley, ST1 3HD
01782 286342

Traditional Bakehouse
250 Uttoxeter Road, Blythe Bridge
01782 395551

Traditional Oatcake Shop
106, Church Street, Stoke, ST4 1DQ
01782 744559

Weston Coyney Oatcakes
12 New Kingsway, Weston Coyney
ST3 6NA, 07516 422908

William Ambrose Oatcake Shop
4 Morris Square, Wolstanton, ST5 0EN
01782 619553

Ye Olde Oatcake Shop
11 Cross Street, Cheadle, ST10 1NP
01538 751393

Compiled from www.theoatcakeguide.co.uk

Notes

1. Pamela Murray, 'Oatbread in North Staffordshire', *Folk Life: a Journal of Ethnological Studies*, vol. 12, 1974, pp. 48–54.

2. *The Sentinel* Friday, 11 January 2008, p. 1.

3. Val Cheke, *Cheese and Butter*, Rupert Hart-Davis, 1956.

4. Andrew Shanahan, 'Canteen Culture', *The Guardian* newspaper, Monday 12 November, 2007.

5. www.poveysoatcakes.com and www.bbc.co.uk/stoke.

6. Laura Mason and Catherine Brown, *Traditional Foods of Britain: an inventory*, prepared for GEIE/Euroterroirs, Prospect Books, 1999, p. 266.

7. John Walton, *Fish and Chips and the British Working Class, 1870–1940*, Leicester University Press, p. 1.

8. Peter Brears, 'The Chekich in England', *Petits Propos Culinaire*, No. 51, 1995, p. 37.

9. Günter Wiegelmann, 'Innovations in Food and Meals', *Folk Life*, vol. 12, 1974, pp. 20–30.

10. S. Minwel Tibbott, *Domestic Life in Wales*, University of Wales Press, 2002, p. 57.

11. David Miles, *The Tribes of Britain*, Weidenfeld and Nicolson, 2005, p. 113.

12. Steven G. Pratt and Kathy Mathews, *SuperFoods HealthStyle*, Bantam Books, 2006, p. 109.

13. www.ceresorganic.com/healthbenefits; Pratt and Mathews, *SuperFoods*, pp. 109–12.

14. N. L. Kent and A. D. Evers, *The Technology of Cereals: an Introduction for Students of Food Science and Agriculture*, Woodhead Publishing, 1993, p. 14.

15. Arthur Hill Hassell, *Food and its Adulterations; comprising the Reports of the Analytical Sanitary Commission of the 'Lancet' for the years 1851 to 1854 inclusive*, Longman, Brown, Green and Longman, 1855, p. 267.

16. Reay Tannahill, *Food in History*, Eyre Methuen, 1973, p. 37.

17. C. Anne Wilson, *Food and Drink in Britain*, Constable, 1973, p. 230.

18. Michael J. Hanson, 'Ducal Estate Management in Georgian Nottinghamshire and Derbyshire: the Diary of William Gould, 1783–1788', *Thoroton Society Record Series*, Vol. 44, 2006.

19. John Burnett, *Plenty and Want: a Social History of Food in England from 1815 to the present day*, first published 1966, Routledge 1989, p. 29.

20. Tibbott, *Domestic Life*, pp. 12–13.

21. Tannahill, *Food in History*, pp. 192–4.

22. Dyer, *Everyday Life*, p. 90; Wilson, *Food and Drink in Britain*, pp. 199–200; for a wide variety of recipes for potages see Peter Brears, *Cooking and Dining in Medieval England*, Prospect Books, pp. 228–92.

23. Tibbott, *Domestic Life*, p. 80.

24. C. Anne Wilson, 'Travellers' Fare: Food encountered by some earlier visitors to the Pennine Region' in *Traditional Food East and West of the Pennines*, ed. C. Anne Wilson, Alan Sutton, 1994, p. 39.

25. Kate Colquhoun, *Taste: the story of Britain through its Cooking*, Bloomsbury, 2007, p. 38; Brears, *Petits Propos Culinaire*, 51, p. 37.

26. F. Atkinson, 'Oatbread in Northern England', *Gwerin*, III, no. 2, 1960, pp. 44–55; Peter Brears, 'Oatcake in the West Riding', *Folk Life*, vol. 12, 1974, pp. 55–9; M. Hartley and J. Ingilby, *Life and Tradition in the Yorkshire Dales*, 1968, pp. 21–8.

27. Harry Speight, *Nidderdale and the garden of the Nidd*, 1894, p. 564.

28. William E. Kapelle, *The Norman Conquest of the North*, Croom Helm, 1979, pp. 214–27.

29. William Scarratt, *Old Times in the Potteries*, 1906, p. 118, noting visits to Barleybat Hall, Cheshire, to collect barley to make into 'ston-cakes'.

30. Hartley and Ingilby, *Life and Tradition*, p. 21.

31. Anne Wilson, *Food and Drink*, p. 258.

32. F. W. Moody, 'Oatbread', in *A Century of Yorkshire Dialect*, eds A. Kellett and I. Dewhurst, Otley, 1997, p. 91; M. Hartley and J. Ingilby, *Making Oatcake*, Smith Settle, 1998.

33. Anne Wilson, *Food and Drink*, p. 24.

34. Anne Wilson., *Food and Drink*, p. 22.

35. Tibbott, *Domestic Life*, pp. 78–86.

36. Robert Plot, *The Natural History of Staffordshire*, 1686, p. 109.

37. R. A. Pelham, 'The 1801 Crop Returns for Staffordshire in their geographical setting', *Collections for a History of Staffordshire*, 1950–51, pp. 231–42, Appendix.

38. Pelham, 'Crop Returns', p. 237.

39. Thomas Brown, *A General View of the Agriculture of the County of Derby*, 1794, p. 19.

40. William Pitt, *A General View of the Agriculture of the County of Stafford*, 1796, pp. 56–7, 201.

41. William Farey, *A General View of the Agriculture of the County of Derby*, 1813, p. 130.

42. David Parsons, Tania Styles and Carole Hough, *The Vocabulary of English Place-Names*, vol. A-Box, Centre for English Name Studies, Nottingham, 1997, p. 59.

43. Moody, 'Oatbread', p. 96.

44. Saddleworth Museum Archives. See also Atkinson, 'Oatbread in Northern England', p. 49.

45. Angus J. L. Winchester, *The Harvest of the Hills: rural life in Northern England and the Scottish Borders, 1400–1700*, Edinburgh University Press, 2000, p. 140.

46. David Horovitz, *The place-names of Staffordshire*, Horovitz, 2005, pp. 75, 79.

47. Hartley and Ingilby, *Life and Tradition*, p. 22: Brears, 'Oatcake', p. 57.

48. Information from the Saddleworth Museum.

49. Farey, *General View*, p. 431.

50. Brears, *Gentlewoman's Kitchen*, p. 67.

51. Information from the Saddleworth Museum.

52. Brears, 'Oatcake', p. 58.

53. E. M. Jope and R. I. Threlfall, 'Excavations of a Medieval Settlement at Beere, North Tawton, Devon', *Medieval Archaeology*, II, 1958, pp. 119–39.

54. Brears, *Gentlewoman's Kitchen*, p. 66; Hartley and Ingilby, *Making Oatcake*, p. 4; Tibbott, *Domestic Life*, p. 81.

55. Thomas Bateman, *Ten Years Diggings in Celtic and Saxon Grave Hills in the counties of Derby, Stafford and York from 1848 to 1858*, George Allen, n.d., p. 199; John Ward, *Romano-British Buildings and Earthworks*, Methuen, 1911, p. 185.

56. Nineteenth-century excavators often attributed Roman dates to later burials. See Barry M. Marsden, *The Early Barrow Diggers*, Tempus, 1999, p. 58.

57. Winchester, *The Harvest of the Hills*, pp. 124–5.

58. Moody, 'Oatbread', p. 92.

59. *English Dialect Dictionary*, ll, p. 28: 'Dashin – a tub used for kneading oatmeal'. This is an inaccurate description for its use, at least in Staffordshire, since the leaven here was not kneaded. EDD gives no Staffordshire reference but quotes a Derbyshire correspondent: 'I have known this word all my life. It is a deep wooden or earthen vessel in which the leaven for oatmeal is "laid". Some of the leaven is left in every week and ferments, forming souring to

raise the next baking.'; C. H. Poole, *An Attempt towards a Glossary of Archaic and Provincial Words of the County of Stafford*, 1880; M. H. Miller, *Old Leeke*, 1891; John Clark, 'Dialect of the Staffordshire Moorlands', *Transactions of the North Staffordshire Field Club*, LIV, 1919–20, p. 44; Dr J. Levitt, unpublished notes deposited at Keele University.

60. *English Dialect Dictionary*, III, p. 472: 'Nakit – a tub for mixing oatcake'. The dictionary gives a single reference from West Yorkshire. See also Brears, *Gentlewoman's Kitchen*, p. 65.

61. *English Dialect Dictionary*, III, p. 70: 'Ark – a large oblong box or chest, divided into compartments, generally two, for keeping corn, meal, etc.'

62. Information from Mr W. Bonsall, West Side, Hulme End, Staffordshire Arts and Museum Service, R.5/73.

63. 'Burnt iron' figures as 'brund iron' or 'brundard', 'brundred' or 'brandart' in other Lichfield inventories, for example, Thomas Adderley of Kingsley, 1725, Eliza Wright of Moddershall, 1725, and Ralph Browne of Caverswall, 1670. *English Dialect Dictionary*, I, p. 377: 'Brandreth – an iron framework placed over or before the fire, on which to rest utensils in cooking.'

64. C. B. Phillips and J. H. Smith, eds, *Stockport Probate Inventories*, vol. 1, Lancashire and Cheshire Record Society, 1984–5, pp. 94–5.

65. John Burnett, *Useful Toil: autobiographies of working people from the 1820s to the 1920s*, Allen Lane, London, 1974, p. 66.

66. Informant aged 92 in 1996 recalling the memories of her father, born in 1870.

67. Author's record of a new farmhouse plan in Hollinsclough, dated 1894.

68. Anne Wilson, *Food and Drink*, p. 237.

69. Staffordshire Arts and Museum Service, R36/73.

70. Staffordshire Arts and Museum Service, R21/70. There are innumerable local variants, including the addition of vinegar, R45/73. Information about bicarbonate of soda from Mrs Beth Sutton.

71. Tibbott, *Domestic Life*, p. 84.

72. Staffordshire Record Office, household account book of Mrs Frances Sherrington of Trentham Hall, D593/R/1/6/4.

73. Staffordshire Record Office, accounts of John Fenton of Shelton Hall, D(W)1788, volume 77.

74. Brears, *Gentlewoman's Kitchen*, p. 65.

75. David Alan Gatley, *Hanley in 1851 revisited: a survey based on the census returns*, Staffordshire University, 1996, p. 12.

76. *The Spencer Report of the Factory*

Commission on Child Employment, 1833; *The Scrivens Report of the Commission on the Employment of Children in the Pottery Industry*, 1841.

77. Stir pudding as an alternative name for hasty pudding, see Mrs A. Johnson, Wheaton Aston, Staffordshire Arts and Museum Service, R55/72. For details of hasty pudding see Anne Wilson, *Food and Drink*, p. 213.

78. William Pitt, *Agriculture of the County of Stafford*, 1796, p. 57.

79. Mason and Brown, *Traditional Foods of Britain*, p. 266, quoting from Sir Humphrey Davy, *Elements of Agricultural Chemistry*, 1813.

80. Staffordshire Record Office. D685/11/3.

81. Peter Higginbotham, *The Workhouse Cookbook*, The History Press, 2008, p. 34.

82. Quoted in Hassell, *Food and its Adulterations*, p. 267.

83. Enoch Wood Collection, Potteries Museum.

84. Mervyn Jones, *Potbank: a social enquiry into life in the Potteries*, Secker and Warburg, 1961, p. 169.

85. Information from Tony Phillips, Keele University.

86. Staffordshire Arts and Museum Service Museum, R6/70.

87. Staffordshire Arts and Museum Service R14/69; R6/70; R19/70; R21/70; R27/73; R29/73; R32/73; R34/73. Also see Miller, *Old Leeke*, II, 1912, p. 32.

88. Staffordshire Arts and Museum Service R29/73.

89. Staffordshire Arts and Museum Service R29/73.

90. Letter to the author dated April, 1995, from an informant who was born in 1930 in Birch Tree, Hanley.

91. J. C. Drummond and Anne Wilbraham, *The Englishman's Food: Five Centuries of English Diet*, first published 1939, Pimlico 1991, p. 449; Burnett, *Plenty and Want*, pp. 291–5.

92. Stephen Mennell, *All Manners of Food*, Basil Blackwell, 1985, p. 249.

93. Staffordshire Arts and Museum Service R8/71, R4/71.

94. Information provided by Mr Graham Bebbington.

95. Information provided by Mr Dave Wright of Wright's Pies.

96. Information provided by Mr Graham Bebbington.

97. Information provided by Mrs Joan Dils.

98. www.poveysoatcakes.com.

99. Staffordshire Arts and Museum Service R4/71.

100. *The Sentinel*, 14 January, 2008, p. 5, col. 5.

101. *The Sentinel*, 29 January, 2008, p. 12, col. 2.

Author's Acknowledgements

I wish to thank the many individuals who have contributed information, memories and photographs to this enterprise. Some of my earliest informants are now dead, but without them all the book would not have been possible. Where appropriate, acknowledgements are in the text or notes. I am especially grateful to all the oatcake-makers who patiently answered my questions.

My thanks are also due to the staff of several public and private institutions: Knights Solicitors, Newcastle-under-Lyme; the Library of the National Museum of Wales; the Potteries Museum; Saddleworth Museum Archives; Staffordshire Arts and Museum Service; Staffordshire and Stoke-on-Trent Archive Service; William Salt Library, Stafford: and to the members of the North Staffordshire Historians Guild who have provided me with ideas, material and encouragement.

I would particularly like to thank: Paul Anderton, Chris Bates, Matthew Blake, Peter Clarkson, Tim Eades, Glen Fowler, Sue Gaukroger, Cliff Guttridge, Sheila Hine, Paul Niblett, Barrie Roberts, Victoria Rowe, Beth Sutton, Jim Sutton, Elspeth Walker, Dave Wright (of Wright's Pies). I also thank those long-suffering friends who have been dragged around on early Sunday morning expeditions to photograph oatcake shops and sample their products; and, of course my gratitude goes to the patient and skilled staff of Carnegie Publishing.

All reasonable attempts have been made to trace copyright holders. Please accept my apologies where I have failed, and contact either myself or the publisher. No doubt I have made many blunders and omissions – all mine, I'm afraid.